LINDLEY M

*Front cover: The Summerhouse which stood in Lindley Murray's garden at Holdgate House. Presented to The Mount School, York in 1901 by William Wilberforce Morrell.*

# The Murrays of New York

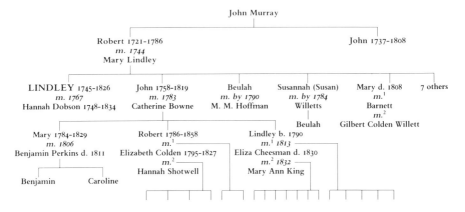

# Lindley Murray
## 1745-1826

### Quaker Grammarian
of
New York and old York

by
Stephen Allott, MA B.LITT.

SESSIONS BOOK TRUST
YORK
1991

ISBN 1 85072 088 6

© Sessions Book Trust 1991

Printed in 10 on 11 point Bembo Typeface
by William Sessions Limited
The Ebor Press
York, England

## Contents

| CHAPTER | | PAGE |
|---|---|---|
| | Genealogy | ii |
| | Foreword | viii |
| | Introduction | xiii |
| I | In His Own Words | 1 |
| | *Notes to Chapter 1* | 34 |
| II | Elizabeth Frank's Account | 39 |
| | *Notes to Chapter 2* | 44 |
| III | In His Correspondence | 46 |
| | *Note to Chapter 3* | 54 |
| IV | Lindley the Friend | 55 |
| | *Notes to Chapter 4* | 64 |
| V | Murray the Grammarian | 66 |
| VI | Excerpts from the Grammar | 71 |
| | *Notes to Chapter 6* | 81 |
| | Index | 85 |

## Illustrations

| | PAGE |
|---|---|
| ★ Silhouette of Lindley Murray | ii |
| ★ Title page of John Gough's *Practical Grammar* | vii |
| ★ Title page of John Gough's *Practical Arithmetic* | x |
| ★★ Page One of 1795 *English Grammar* | xi |

| | | |
|---|---|---|
| †† | Three young teachers on their way to Holdgate House | xii |
| † | Letter to John Murray in New York regarding finance | 24 |
| ★★ | 1795 English Grammar title page | 28 |
| # | 1808 English Grammar title page | 32 |
| †† | Lindley Murray's chair | 38 |
| ‡ | Lindley Murray | 39 |
| †† | Lindley Murray's desk | 41 |
| ‡ | Title page of 'The Power of Religion on the Mind' 1825 | 43 |
| ‡ | Electioneering pamphlet by William Tuke, Thomas Priestman and Lindley Murray for William Wilberforce | 45 |
| † | Letter to John Murray of New York regarding Mary Perkin's ailment | 47 |
| ‡ | Title page of 'A Compendium of Religious Faith & Practice' 1815 | 51 |
| †† | Residence of Lindley Murray from the road | 53 |
| †† | Holdgate House from the garden, 1827 | 54 |
| ‡ | Proposed Boarding School for Girls at York | 57 |
| †† | Lindley Murray's Summerhouse | 63 |
| ‡ | Title page of 'The Principles of Religion' 1805 | 65 |
| ‡ | The Sound of the Consonants | 70 |
| ★ | Silhouette of Lindley Murray | 84 |
| | Traditionally the Seal of Lindley Murray (by courtesy of Paula Procter) | 86 |

★ By permission of the Library Committee of London Yearly Meeting of the Religious Society of Friends

★★ Courtesy of Leeds University Library

† By permission of the Haviland Records Room, the Archives of New York Yearly Meeting of the Religious Society of Friends

†† Courtesy of The Archives, The Mount School, York

‡ From William Sessions Limited Archives

# By courtesy The Minster Library, York

# A Practical Grammar
## OF THE
## *Englijh Tongue.*

CONTAINING

The Most MATERIAL RULES and OBSERVATIONS for underſtanding the *ENGLISH* Language WELL, and writing it with PROPRIETY.

### IN FIVE PARTS.

I. ORTHOGRAPHY, or the Art of SPELLING; a Introductory to which are prefixed ſundry new ORTHOGRAPHICAL TABLES.

II. ANALOGY, which treats of the ſeveral PARTS of SPEECH.

III. ETYMOLOGY, or the DERIVATION of WORDS.

IV. SYNTAX, or RULES for joining WORDS rightly in a SENTENCE.

V. PROSODY, or RULES for PRONUNCIATION.

For the USE of S C H O O L S.

Firſt compiled by *J A M E S G O U G H.* Reviſed, digeſted and enlarged with ſundry material Rules by *J O H N G O U G H,* of *Cole-Alley, DUBLIN.*

The Third EDITION, with many ADDITIONS.

*Quicquid præcipies eſto brevis ; ut cito dicta*
*Percipiant animi dociles, teneantque fideles.*

Short be thy Rules, that ſo the ſtudious Young
With Eaſe may learn them, and retain them long.

D U B L I N:
Printed by ISAAC JACKSON: And ſold by ſeveral of the Bookſellers, for the Authors *James Gough* in *Briſtol*; and *John Gough* aforeſaid, by whom Bookſellers, or Subſcribers may be furniſhed. 1764.

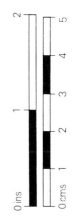

Title page of John Gough's 'Practical Grammar'.

# Foreword
by Malcolm Thomas
Librarian of Friends House, Euston Road, London

LINDLEY MURRAY is not a household name; but he once was. His *Grammar* and *English Reader* were reprinted and used on both sides of the Atlantic (and beyond), and not only by Quakers. In this respect he is comparable to John Gough, the Dublin Quaker schoolmaster, whose *Practical Grammar* was superseded by Murray's though Gough's *Practical Arithmetic* still remained a standard work for many years. Perhaps no textbook writer is a hero to the pupils of his day, and Stephen Allott notes John Dalton's reservations on the *Grammar*, shared by John Bright when he remembered his days at Ackworth School. Anne Ogden Boyce in the 1880s looked back at the 'children who, 50 years ago, toiled over the large and small print of his octavo Grammar, [and] found it a somewhat weary pilgrimage through which the examples in Prosody looked like the Delectable Mountains at the end of the journey'. But she also reminds us that when 'we take up his "Reader", and imagine little Friends making acquaintance with "Damon and Pythias", with "Cicero against Verres", and "Adherbal against Jugurtha", and with the poetry and prose of Goldsmith and Addison, we need not wonder at the honour in which Lindley Murray was held by young and old'.

John Stephenson Rowntree, writing of Bootham School, gives us an idea of the chronological limit of Murray's influence: '. . . in 1865 the *Sequel* was laid aside as a reading-book. It had survived *The English Reader* five years. The *Introduction* sustains a lingering existence, but the present generation of school-boys is almost ignorant of those compilations of Lindley Murray's with which their fathers were so familiar. His *Grammar* was gradually superseded after 1860'.

Murray's reputation extended far beyond Friends, not only because of the utility of his writings, but because – as Stephen Allott points out – they were essentially undenominational, bearing few of the outward and distinctive marks of Quakerism. In *The Power of Religion on the Mind* he assembled 'a collection of testimonies of great and good persons in favour of piety and virtue. . . . And I wished to form it upon liberal principles, and render it acceptable to readers in general, I was careful to introduce characters of various religious professions, and of different ages and countries'. This style was reflected in his manners. Professor Silliman of Yale, visiting him in 1805, described his conversation as 'modest, gentle, easy, and persuasive . . . Mr Murray belongs to the Society of Friends, but both he and Mrs Murray have so tempered the strictness of the manners peculiar to their Society, that they are polished people, with the advantage of the utmost simplicity of deportment'.

In 1819 we find Mary Capper visiting Quaker families and recommending two works in particular to parents: Henry Tuke's *Principles of Religion* and Murray's *Compendium*. Like his friend Tuke, whose work he edited and whose memoir he wrote, Murray embodied a style and theology so appropriate for its day that after being best-sellers his writings went into an abrupt decline in Britain (though not in the United States). He stands with Tuke, Stephen Grellet, and William Forster as early Quaker-evangelicals; but we should remember that John Wilbur also thought well of him. He was not evangelical enough for the later 19th century, but too evangelical for liberal theology. Like Tuke and Grellet he was politically conservative: he settled in England 'because I was ever partial to its political constitution, and the mildness and wisdom of its general system of laws. I knew that under this excellent government, life, property, reputation, civil and religious liberty, are happily protected'. It is no surprise to find him a zealous supporter of Pitt, and encouraging Friends to vote for William Wilberforce as MP for the county of York in 1807. This was on humanitarian – antislavery – as well as Tory principles. Although an invalid for most of his life in England, he was still active – giving legal advice to the Lothersdale Quakers imprisoned in York for refusal to pay tithes, and involved in founding The Retreat, in antislavery work, and in the York schools. It was no wonder that he was for 40 years one of the landmarks for Quaker and non-Quaker visitors to York. His charm, like Wilberforce's, needed to be experienced and is now elusive; but his life and writings – particularly his autobiography – tell us much about the thought and feeling of his day which we are poorer for having forgotten.

# PRACTICAL ARITHMETICK

## IN FOUR BOOKS.

I. WHOLE NUMBERS, WEIGHTS and MEASURES.
II. FRACTIONS, VULGAR and DECIMAL.
III. MERCANTILE ARITHMETICK.
IV. EXTRACTIONS, PROGRESSIONS, LOGARITHMS, &c.

EXTRACTED FROM

The Larger, Entire Treatife, carried on by Subfcription, and Adapted to the Commerce of *Ireland*, as well as that of *Great-Britain*.

*For the Ufe of SCHOOLS.*

By *J. Gough.*

LONDON:
Printed for S. HOOPER, No. 25. LUDGATE-HILL.
MDCCLXXIII.

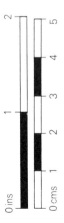

Title page of Gough's 'Practical Arithmetic'.

# ENGLISH GRAMMAR, &c.

ENGLISH GRAMMAR is the art of fpeaking and writing the Englifh language with propriety.
It is divided into four parts, viz. Orthography, Etymology, Syntax, and Profody.

## OF ORTHOGRAPHY.

#### LETTERS.

Orthography teaches the nature and powers of letters, and the juft method of fpelling words.

A letter is the firft principle, or leaft part, of a word.

The letters of the Englifh language, called the Englifh Alphabet, are twenty-fix in number.

B

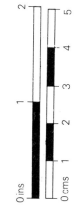

*Page one of the first edition of Lindley Murray's English Grammar, 1795.*

*A visit to Lindley Murray's house by the three young teachers from Esther Tuke's School in Trinity Lane (wearing their pattens).*

# Introduction

ON A WINTER EVENING, about the year 1790, three young Quaker women might have been seen passing out of Micklegate Bar in York, attended by a man carrying a lantern. They were on their way to the village of Holgate, a mile outside the city walls, for a lesson in English Grammar from the American Quaker lawyer, Lindley Murray, who had settled there in the hope that the cool Yorkshire climate might help his ailing health. They came from the Quaker girls' school, established in Trinity Lane in 1784 by Esther Tuke; their lessons were the origin of Murray's English Grammar, which Blackwood's Magazine was to declare in 1839 'reigns despotically through young ladies' schools from the Orkneys to the Cornish Scillys'.

The number of English grammars published had increased in the late 18th century, and Lindley Murray borrowed freely from his predecessors, for he made little claim to originality. Yet his was the one which met the needs of the time and became the standard text-book. In its abridged form 112 editions were published, the last in 1877, while the full-length work had 58 editions in England between 1794 and 1867, besides many in America. It was remarked that 'Murray' became a synonym for grammar, as 'Euclid' was for geometry, and that one could as well speak of 'Murray's English' as of 'King's English', such was his influence on the way English was spoken and written in the 19th century.

The account which he wrote of his early years in America and of his most productive period as a writer in England is our chief source of knowledge of him. It was published in a memoir in the year of his death, 1826, by his friend and admirer, Elizabeth Frank, who added her own version of the rest of his life. It is also the principal surviving example of the English style which he advocated and has an 18th century Quaker charm, not unlike that of John Woolman's Journal. It therefore forms the main part of this book, in a somewhat shortened form, and is followed by a summary of Elizabeth Frank's account, with further information based on Quaker archives both in Yorkshire and in New York. Assessments of him as a typical Friend of his period and as a grammarian are followed by excerpts from the Grammar, which illustrate the language and thought with which his pupils had to cope, and make points on style and grammar still relevant today.

I am particularly grateful to Professor David A. Reibel of the University of Tubingen for permission to use both his edited version and the original of C. E. West's MA thesis, *Lindley Murray, Grammarian* (1953), both unpublished; also for the generous help of their expertise and resources to Elizabeth H. Moger, Archivist of the Haviland Records Room of New York Yearly Meeting, and to Malcolm Thomas, Librarian of the Central Library of London Yearly Meeting, both of the Religious Society of Friends; to Michael Thompson M.B., B.S.; to Frederick A. Davies, Archivist of Ackworth School; The Mount School, York, where Lindley Murray's chair is still in use in the Head's room and where his summerhouse still stands in their grounds. Also to Paula (Procter) Lambert, their Archivist, for illustrations and sight of Lindley Murray's desk and the seal, traditionally believed by her family to belong to the Grammarian; to Rita Freedman, York City Archivist; to Bernard Barr of York Minster Library; to the Borthwick Institute for Historical Research (University of York); and to P. S. Morrish, Sub-Librarian of Leeds University Library. Finally my thanks go to William K. and E. Margaret Sessions for their encouragement and for the use of illustrations from their *Tukes of York* and books in their archives.

CHAPTER I

# In His Own Words
### Including his own punctuation and spelling

I WAS BORN in the year 1745 at Swetara, near Lancaster,[1] in the state of Pennsylvania. My parents were of respectable characters, and in the middle station of life. My father[2] possessed a good flour mill at Swetara:[3] but being of an enterprising spirit, and anxious to provide handsomely for his family, he made several voyages to the West Indies in the way of trade, by which he considerably augmented his property. Pursuing his inclinations, he, in time, acquired large possessions, and became one of the most respectable merchants in America.

In the pursuit of business, he was steady and indefatigable. During the middle period of his life, he had extensive concerns in ships; and was engaged in a variety of other mercantile affairs. But this great and multifarious employment, never appeared to agitate or oppress his mind: he was distinguished for equanimity and composure. And I have often heard it remarked, that, by his conversation and deportment, no person would have imagined, that he had such a weight of care upon him. When in the company of his friends, he was so thoroughly unbent, that persons unacquainted with the nature and variety of his business, might naturally suppose that he had very little employment. This trait may be justly considered as an evidence of strong powers of mind. These had been cultivated by attention to business, and by much intercourse with the world. But my father did not possess the advantages of a liberal education; by which his talents and virtues might have been still more extensively useful.

My mother[4] was a woman of an amiable disposition and remarkable for mildness, humanity and liberality of sentiment. She was, indeed, a faithful and affectionate wife, a tender mother, and a kind mistress. I recollect, with emotions of affection and gratitude, her unwearied solicitude for my health and happiness. This excellent mother died some years after I had been settled in life. And though I had cause to mourn for the loss of her, yet I had reason to be thankful to Divine Providence, that I had been blessed with her for so long a period, and particularly through the dangerous seasons of childhood and youth.

Both my parents, who belonged to the Society of Friends, were concerned to promote the religious welfare of their children. They often gave us salutary admonition, and trained us up to attend the public worship of God. The Holy Scriptures were read in the family: a duty which, when regularly and devoutly performed, must be fraught with the most beneficial effects. I recollect being, at one time, in a situation of the room, where I observed that my father, on reading these inspired volumes to us, was so much affected as to shed tears. . .

Our family was rather numerous. My parents had twelve children, of whom I was the eldest. But the course of time has reduced us to a small number. At the present period, (the summer of 1806,) only four of us remain.

That activity of body, for which I was remarkable in youth and mature life, commenced at an early age. When I was only nine[5] months old, I frequently escaped, as I have been informed, from the care of the family; and, unnoticed by them, made my way from the house to the mill, which were more than a hundred yards distant from each other. As soon as I could run about, I proved to be, not only an active, but a mischievous child. I played many tricks, which did not denote the best disposition, and which gave a wrong bias to my vivacity. This perverse turn of mind might have been checked in the bud, if it had received suitable, early correction.

But I had a very fond grandmother, with whom I was a great favourite, and who often protected me from proper chastisement, when I richly deserved it. . . The irregular[6] vivacity which I possessed, received, however, a very salutary control, by my being afterwards placed under the care of a discreet and sensible aunt, who was determined to bring me into some degree of order and submission. The great indulgence with which I had been treated, must have rendered the contest rather severe: for, on a particular occasion, I embraced the opportunity of getting out of a window, and running about on the roof of a small tenement; which was, however, so high, that a fall would have endangered my life. My aunt was in great distress; and I believe endeavoured, but in vain, to influence my fears, and, by this means, induce me to return. I moved about for a while, in this perilous situation, and probably enjoyed my temporary independence. She, at last, with great prudence, entreated me very tenderly to come to her. But though this affected me, I did not comply till I had obtained her promise, that I should not be corrected. She kept her word; but I think she did not relax, in any degree, the general rigour of her discipline towards me. I was at length completely subdued, and brought into regular obedience: and this event[7] proved comfortable to myself, as well as relieving to everyone that had any care of me. . .

At an early period, about my sixth or seventh year,[8] I was sent to the city of Philadelphia, that I might have the advantage of a better school than the country afforded. I well remember being some time at the academy of Philadelphia, the English department of which was then conducted by the truly respectable Ebenezer Kinnersley. He exercised great care over his pupils: and from what I recollect of this instructer [sic] of youth, and what I have read of him, I have reason to regret, that my continuance in that seminary was of short duration. I remember to have read there with pleasure, even at that age, some passages in 'The Travels of Cyrus'; and to have been agreeably exercised in the business of parsing sentences.

From this academy I was taken, to accompany my parents to North Carolina. My father conceived, that some commercial advantages would attend a temporary residence in that province. When I first landed there, I was much delighted with roving about, after a long confinement on ship board. In one of these little excursions, I found a few shillings; which were readily expended in some loaves of bread, for the refreshment of the sailors. These people had been kind to me during the voyage; and I could not therefore, think of any more pleasing application of my treasure, than in treating them with some excellent fresh bread. Their grateful acceptance, and enjoyment, of this little gift, was doubtless a rich reward for my attention to them.

In the year 1753,[9] my father left Carolina; and, with his family, settled at New York. In this city I was placed at a good school, in which I made the usual progress of young learners. Being extremely fond of play, I believe I rarely neglected any opportunity of indulging this propensity. At the times of vacation, I generally enjoyed myself with diversions, till the period for returning to school approached. I then applied myself vigorously to the task that had been previously assigned me; and I do not recollect that I ever failed to perform it, to the satisfaction of my teacher. A heedless boy, I was far from reflecting, how much more prudent it would have been, if I had, in the first place, secured the lesson, and afterwards indulged myself in my playful pursuits. . . Sometimes I absented myself from school, to enjoy a greater degree of play and amusement. During these pleasures, the idea of impending correction, would occasionally come across my mind: but I resolutely repelled it, as an intruder which would unnecessarily imbitter [sic] my present enjoyment.

About this period, a very happy impression was made on my mind, by a piece which was given me to write, and in the performance of which I had to exhibit a specimen of my best handwriting. The sheet was decorated round its edges with a number of pleasing figures, displayed with taste and simplicity. In the centre, my performance was to be contained. This was a transcript of the visit and salutation of the angels to the shepherds, near Bethlehem, who were tending their flocks by night. The beauty of the sheet; the property I was to have in it; and the distinction which I expected from performing the work in a handsome manner; prepared my mind for relishing the solemn narrative, and the interesting language of the angels to the shepherds. I was highly pleased with the whole. The impression was so strong and delightful, that it has often occurred to me, through life, with great satisfaction; and, at this hour, it is remembered with pleasure. . .

I had a curious propensity to discover and observe the natural dispositions of animals.[10] And this curiosity was, in some instances, so strong as to make me overlook the uneasiness which, by teasing them, was occasioned to the animals themselves. I was not naturally of a cruel disposition; but was rather pleased to see the animal creation about me, enjoy themselves. The propensity I have mentioned was, however, sometimes unwarrantably indulged: so much so, as to mark a depraved turn of mind, which, even now, gives me pain to recollect. . .

The unwarrantable curiosity which I have just mentioned, continued to operate, in some degree, for many years; and, occasionally, showed itself long after I was grown up. I recollect a particular instance of it, which was very near proving fatal to me; and which, though a little out of the course of my narrative, may not improperly be related in this place. . .

When I was in England, in the year 1771, I went to see the elephants, which were kept at the Queen's stables, Buckingham-house. Whilst I was gratifying myself with observing the huge creatures, and their various actions and peculiarities, I took occasion to withdraw from one of them a part of the hay, which he was collecting on the floor with his proboscis. I did this with my cane; and watched the animal very narrowly, to prevent a stroke from him, which I had reason to expect. The keeper said that I had greatly displeased the elephant, and that he would never forget the injury. I thought but little of this admonition at the time. But about six weeks afterwards, when I accompanied some other persons on a visit to the elephants, I found that, though probably several hundred people had been there since my preceding visit, the animal soon recognised me. I did not attempt to molest or tease him at all; and I had no conception of any concealed resentment. On a sudden, however, when I was supposed to be within reach of his proboscis, he threw it towards me with such violence, that if it had struck me, I should probably have been killed, or have received some material injury. Happily for me, I perceived his intention, and being very active, I sprung out of his reach. To every other person present, he was gentle and good-tempered; and his enmity to me arose, as the keeper declared, solely from the circumstance of the little affront which I had formerly put upon him. . .

At an early age, I was placed in the counting house of my father, who was desirous of training me to the mercantile profession. I did not, however, relish this employ, and the confinement to which it subjected me. I wished to be any thing rather than a merchant. And this, perhaps, may be accounted for, by the strictness with which I was kept to business, and the undue restraints as I conceived, which were put, at that early period, on my lively spirits and allowable indulgences. My father kept steady to his purpose. He probably thought that my dislike to the business would, in time, abate. He sent me to Philadelphia, influenced, perhaps, by a hope, that a residence with a merchant at a distance from home, would better reconcile me to the employment.[11] But this expedient did not answer his expectation; and, after some time, he consented to my return to New York.

About this period, I contracted a taste for reading, and a desire for a greater degree of literary improvement. The pleasures of study, and the advantages and distinctions, which learning and knowledge had conferred on individuals who fell under my observation, augmented my wishes for the acquisition of science and literature. Another experiment was, however, made to reconcile me to mercantile life. My father presented me with a considerable number of silver watches, which he designed as a little trading stock; and which he had just imported, with many other articles, from England. By having the property of these watches, and by the prospect of increasing that property on the sale of them, and thus extending my concerns, in fresh purchases with the product,[12] I began to relish the occupation. The spirit of trading took hold of me; and I contemplated, with pleasure, the future enlargement of my funds. In short, I entered into the business with ardour and satisfaction. At the same time I continued in my father's counting house; and occasionally assisted in the routine of his commercial affairs. I doubt not, that he surveyed this success of his schemes for my advantage, with peculiar complacency.[13] But not long after the commencement of my trading engagements, an incident occurred, which seemed to blast all his expectations, and to threaten the most serious consequences to myself. . .

Though my father . . . had an earnest desire to promote my interest and happiness, yet he appeared to me, in some respects, and on some occasions, rather too rigorous. Among other regulations, he had, with true parental prudence, given me general directions not to leave the house, in an evening, without previously obtaining his approbation. I believe that his permission was generally and readily procured. But a particular incident occurred, in which, on account of his absence, I could not apply to him. I was invited by an uncle to spend the evening with him; and trusting to this circumstance, and to the respectability of my company, I ventured to break the letter, though I thought not the spirit, of the injunction which had been laid upon me. The next morning, I was taken by my father, into a private apartment, and remonstrated with for my disobedience. In vain were my apologies. Nothing that I could offer, was considered as an extenuation of my having broken a plain and positive command. In short, I received a very severe chastisement; and was threatened with a repetition of it, for every similar offence. Being a lad of some spirit, I felt very indignant at such treatment, under circumstances which, as I conceived, admitted of so much alleviation. I could not bear it; and I resolved to leave my father's house, and seek, in a distant country, what I conceived to be an asylum, or a better fortune. Young and ardent, I did not want confidence in my own powers; and I presumed that, with health and strength which I possessed in a superior degree, I could support myself, and make my way happily through life. I meditated on my plan; and came to the resolution of taking my books and all my property with me, to a town in the interior of the country; where I had understood there was an excellent seminary, kept by a man of distinguished talents and learning. Here I purposed to remain, till I had learned the French language, which I thought would be of great use to me; and till I had acquired as much other improvement as my funds would admit. With this stock of knowledge, I presumed that I should set out in life under much greater advantages, than I should possess by entering immediately into business, with my small portion of property, and great inexperience. I was then about fourteen years of age. My views being thus arranged, I procured a new suit of clothes, entirely different from those which I had been accustomed to wear, packed up my little all, and left the city, without exciting any suspicion of my design, till it was too late to prevent its accomplishment.

In a short time I arrived at the place of destination. I settled myself immediately as a boarder in the seminary, and commenced my studies. The prospect which I entertained was so luminous and cheering, that, on the whole, I did not regret the part I had acted. Past recollections and future hopes combined to animate me. The chief uneasiness which I felt in my present situation, must have arisen from the reflection of having lost the society and attentions of a most affectionate mother, and of having occasioned sorrow to her feeling mind. But as I had passed the Rubicon, and believed I could not be comfortable at home, I contented myself with the thought, that the pursuit of the objects before me, was better calculated than any other, to produce my happiness. In this quiet retreat, I had as much enjoyment as my circumstances were adapted to convey. The pleasure of study, and the glow of a fond imagination, brightened the scenes around me. And the consciousness of a state of freedom and independence, undoubtedly contributed to augment my gratifications, and to animate my youthful heart. But my continuance in this delightful situation, was not of long duration. Circumstances of an apparently trivial nature, concurred to overturn the visionary fabric I had formed, and to bring me again to the paternal roof.

I had a particular friend, a youth about my own age, who resided at Philadelphia. I wished to pay him a short visit, and then resume my studies. We met according to appointment, at an inn on the road. I enjoyed his society, and communicated to him my situation and views. But before I returned to my retreat, an occurrence took place which occasioned me to go to Philadelphia. When I was about to leave that city, as I passed through one of the streets, I met a gentleman who had some time before dined at my father's house. He expressed great pleasure on seeing me; and inquired when I expected to leave the city. I told him I was then on the point of setting off. He thought the occasion very fortunate for him. He had just been with a letter to the postoffice; but found that he was too late. The letter, he said, was of importance; and he begged that I would deliver it with my own hand, and as soon as I arrived at New York, to the person for whom it was directed. Surprised by the request, and unwilling to state to him my situation, I engaged to take good care of the letter.

My new residence was at Burlington,[14] about twenty miles from Philadelphia. I travelled towards it rather pensive, and uncertain what plan to adopt respecting the letter. I believe that I sometimes thought of putting it into the postoffice; sometimes, of hiring a person to deliver it. But the confidence that had been reposed in me; the importance of the trust; and my tacit engagement to deliver it personally; operated so powerfully on my mind, that after I had rode[15] a few miles, I determined, whatever risk and expense I might incur, to hire a carriage for the purpose, to go to New York as speedily as possible, deliver the letter, and return immediately. My design, so far as it respected the charge of the letter, was completely accomplished. I delivered it, according to the direction, and my own engagement. I was, however, obliged to remain in New York that night, as the packet boat, in which I had crossed the bay, could not sail till the next morning. This was a mortifying circumstance, as I wished to return very expeditiously. The delay was, however, unavoidable. I put up at an inn, near the wharf from which the packet was to sail in the morning, and waited for that period with some anxiety.

I thought I had conducted my business with so much caution, that no one acquainted with me, had known of my being in the city. I had, however, been noticed by some person who knew me; and, in the evening, to my great surprise, my uncle, whom I have mentioned before, paid me a visit. He treated me affectionately, and with much prudent attention; and, after some time, strenuously urged me to go with him to my father's house: but I firmly refused to comply with his request. At length he told me, that my mother was greatly distressed on account of my absence; and that I should be unkind and undutiful, if I did not see her. This made a strong impression upon me. I resolved, therefore, to spend a short time with her, and then return to my lodgings. The meeting which I had with my dear and tender parent was truly affecting to me. Everything that passed, evinced the great affection she had for me, and the sorrow into which my departure from home had plunged her. After I had been some time in the house, my father unexpectedly came in; and my embarrassment, under these circumstances, may easily be conceived. It was, however, instantly removed, by his approaching me in the most affectionate manner. He saluted me very tenderly; and expressed great satisfaction on seeing me again. Every degree of resentment was immediately dissipated. I felt myself happy, in perceiving the pleasure which my society could afford to persons so intimately connected with me, and to whom I was so much indebted. We spent the evening together in love and harmony: and I abandoned entirely, without a moment's hesitation, the idea of leaving a house and family, which were now dearer to me than ever.

The next day, a person was sent to the place of my retreat, to settle all accounts, and to bring back my property. I was taken into still greater favour than formerly; and was never reproached by my parents, for the trouble and anxiety which I had brought upon them. My father probably perceived that I felt sufficiently on the occasion; and he was, perhaps, conscious, that the discipline he had exerted, was not altogether justifiable. . .

Before I quit this subject, I must observe, that soon after I had left home, inquiries were made to discover the place to which I had retreated. I knew that this was the case; but I had made up my mind not to return, and subject myself again to a treatment which I had felt to be improper and unmerited. I therefore declined all the proposals and entreaties of individuals who were friends to the family, and who endeavoured to shake the resolutions I had formed. And I am persuaded that, at this period, nothing would have induced me to relinquish them, but a security against the repetition of the harsh discipline which I had experienced. I rejoice, however, that a train of events so unexpected, and so contrary to my fixed purposes, happily brought me again to the paternal mansion, and settled me safely under its protection.

A short time after I had returned to my father's family, I solicited the privilege of having a private tutor, to instruct me in classical knowledge and liberal studies. With this request, my father very generously complied. A tutor of talents and learning, was procured for me: and I pursued this new career with great alacrity of mind. I sat up late, and rose early, in the prosecution of my studies. In the cold season of the year, I had fuel brought at night into my study, that I might have it ready for kindling a fire at the time of rising, which was frequently before daylight. My tutor was very attentive, and gave me great encouragement to persevere. He stimulated my application, by portraying the advantages of science, and by the commendations which he bestowed on my progress. This close attention to study, and confinement to the house, did not, however, agree with my constitution. My sickly hue proclaimed the intenseness of my application. I found it necessary, therefore, to abate the ardency of my pursuit, and to intermix bodily exercise with my studies. This procedure had a happy effect. I continued regularly employed in my literary occupation, and could not but be pleased with the advancement I had made, with the augmentation of knowledge, and the improvement of my mental powers.

It is, however, proper to observe, that my attainments under this tutor, were very limited. They served, indeed, to improve my taste, and increase my desire, for learning and knowledge. But this taste and desire were not, at any future period of my life, accompanied by that ardour and steadiness of pursuit, which often ensure great success: and my stock of knowledge and literary improvement has, consequently, been always far from extensive.

Though I was a youth of great vivacity, and, by my imprudence and love of pleasure, I had been led into many follies and transgressions; yet I always entertained a high opinion of the enjoyments which piety and virtue bestow; and I venerated the character of those whom I deemed to be truly religious. . .

But whatever might be my follies and actual deviations from the line of rectitude, my principles were never disturbed by infidelity[16] or scepticism. I always had the happiness, since I was capable of reflecting on the subject, of having my sentiments fixed in favour of the Christian religion; and no argument that I ever met with, in company or books, had any injurious effects upon me. Some of my acquaintance were either deists or sceptics: but I always found replies to their reasonings, which perfectly satisfied my own mind. This happy persuasion I attribute, under Divine Providence, to my having occasionally looked into, early in life, Leland's View of the Deistical Writers; Butler's Analogy of Religion, Natural and Revealed, to the Constitution and Course of Nature; Sherlock on Providence; and Sherlock's Discourses. These books, with some others, were the means of communicating to my mind, such a survey of the Christian religion and the Divine economy, that I was never much, if at all, embarrassed, by the plausible schemes and objections, which men of prejudiced minds and short-sighted views of religion, had fabricated and produced. I am firmly persuaded that the perplexity and doubts, with regard to Christianity and its evidences, which many sensible and well-disposed minds have encountered, and the absolute infidelity of others, may be fairly attributed to the scanty information which they received, on these subjects, during the period of their education, or that by which it was immediately succeeded.

Not long after I had commenced my studies under a private tutor, I entered into a society of young persons, for the purpose of debating on subjects of importance and difficulty, and of exercising ourselves in the art of elocution. The society met weekly; and as the members knew the subject that would be considered at their next meeting, they had opportunity of preparing themselves for the discussion. I generally employed a considerable portion of this preparatory time, in reading books on the question; in reflecting attentively upon it; in collecting the various arguments which bore upon the subject; in considering objections, with the answers to them; and in disposing the whole into some method and order. This institution enlarged my stock of knowledge, promoted the business of arranging my ideas, and probably produced a small degree of correctness and fluency of expression. . .

As my mind improved, and my views enlarged, I became still more attached to literary pursuits; and the study of the law particularly attracted my attention. When I was about seventeen or eighteen years of age, I expressed this inclination to my father: but it met with his decided opposition; and he took great pains to divert my thoughts from the subject. He represented the temptations which I should have to encounter in the practice of the law; and which, he said, would probably lead me to deviate from the principles and conduct of that religious society of which I was a member. He displayed the advantages I should possess, both in point of emolument and respectability, by the situation in which he was able to place me, as a merchant; and earnestly entreated me to relinquish all prospects of a mode of life, to which there were attached so many difficulties; and to bend my inclinations towards an employment which, I must know, promised almost certain success. I believe I was properly sensible of my father's wishes to establish me advantageously in the world; and of the concern it gave him, to perceive my rooted objection to an occupation, which he very justly considered as both lucrative and honourable. But I found that my inclination was not to be controlled by motives of interest; and though I did not then urge the point, I kept my object steadily in view. After some time had elapsed, I applied myself again vigorously to the subject: but I adopted a new mode of proceeding. I stated the case at large, in writing. My dissatisfaction with the mercantile employment, however beneficial and respectable it might be, and my earnest desire for a literary profession, were fully set forth. All the arguments which I could muster in support of this propensity, and the benefits which it was likely to produce, were enumerated; and every objection which had been advanced against my views and wishes, was distinctly brought forward, and such answers given to the whole, as I thought were satisfactory.

    This little performance, which contained several pages, was shown to my father; it was also occasionally shown to some of our friends, particularly to a gentleman of the law, Benjamin Kissam, Esq. who was my father's counsellor, and a man of eminence and integrity in his profession. The statement had a most favourable effect. The counsellor himself became my advocate: and, in a short time, my father consented to place me under his care and tuition. A considerable sum of money was advanced to him by my father as a fee for initiating me, in the business of my new and favourite occupation, and I entered into it with great alacrity. Time now rolled on very pleasantly; and the hope of being settled in a profession adapted to my wishes, gilded my future prospects. After some time, my father very generously presented me with an excellent library, which comprehended both books of law, and some parts of general literature; and which were well calculated to aid and invigorate my studies. I cannot, however, say that I always found the study of the law to be pleasant. It contains many barren and uninviting tracts, and extensive fields of laborious employment. It abounds with discordant views, with intricate and perplexing discussions, and requires much deep and patient investigation. But I was not discouraged with my occupation. It was the profession of my own choice: it was a respectable business and it promised to afford me a competent support. . .

After four years from the commencement of my law studies, in the office of my truly respectable instructer [sic], I was called to the bar;[17] and received a license to practise, both as counsel and attorney, according to the custom of that time, in all the courts of the province of New York. I soon commenced business, and prosecuted it with success. It answered the expectations I had formed; and I believe my family and friends were satisfied with the prospects which attended me.

Before I entered into business, and about the twentieth year of my age, I conceived a strong attachment and affection for a young woman[18] of personal attractions, good sense, a most amiable disposition, and of a worthy and respectable family. It was not long, before I perceived that my regard met with a favourable reception. Time, and opportunity of knowing each other, confirmed our attachment; and after two years' acquaintance we had the satisfaction of being united in the tender bonds of marriage.[19]

We have lived together more than forty years; and through the whole course of that period, she has been to me a truly affectionate and excellent wife. In all our varied conditions of life, I have received from her the most unequivocal proofs of attachment, and solicitude for my welfare. During my long confinement, on account of bodily infirmities, she has cheerfully met our privations; tenderly sympathized with me; and been cordially disposed to forego her own ease, to afford me assistance and comfort. She has, indeed, been a great blessing to me; and I have abundant cause to be deeply thankful to God, for this unmerited favour, and its continuance to the present time. . .

Not long after I had commenced business, some circumstances rendered it proper for me to make a voyage to England; where my father had been about a year on commercial matters of importance, which made his presence there, at that time, very expedient. For many years previous to his leaving America, he had been considerably indisposed: at the best his constitution was but delicate. The climate of England, however, proved very beneficial. I found him so much improved in his general health, that I could not but wish that he would continue in this country for a few years: and he was so strongly impressed with the hope of receiving benefit, by such a residence, as well as by the advantages which would result to his concerns in trade, that he communicated his views to my mother, and expressed his wish to see her and his children in England.

They accordingly, in the course of a few months, came to him: and as I did not expect to return very soon, my wife was persuaded to accompany them across the Atlantic. I had therefore the comfort and satisfaction of meeting again my beloved wife, mother, brother and sisters.[20] The whole family, thus met together, in a country so distant from their native shores, could not but feel themselves highly gratified, and peculiarly attached to one another. My dear mother was sensible of the improved state of my father's health; and cheerfully consented to reside a few years in England, for its complete establishment.

When I first came to this country, I had not fixed any time for my continuance in it: but soon after my arrival, it appeared probable that, in the course of a year, I should return to America. There was not, therefore, much opportunity for my dear partner and myself to gratify our curiosity, in surveying what was instructive and interesting in this highly cultivated and happy land. We, however, made a good use of our time; and were much pleased with the novelty and information, which, on every side, continually pressed for attention. It was a peculiar gratification to me, that in these excursions and surveys, I had the society of one, in whose entertainment and instruction I felt myself warmly interested. Every enjoyment was, I believe, heightened to both of us, by the consciousness of each other's participation.

In the latter part of the year 1771, we returned to New York. My parents and the rest of the family remained in England several years. But after this period of trial, my father perceived, that the benefit which he derived from the change of climate, was only temporary. His former indisposition resumed its wonted strength. Having therefore arranged his mercantile affairs entirely to his satisfaction, he, with his family, embarked for New York; and arrived safely there, in the year 1775.

With regard to myself, I observe that, on my return to New York, I resumed the practice of the law. I had many friends and connexions; which renewed the pleasing hopes I had formerly possessed, of succeeding in business. Attention and industry were not wanting; and I enjoyed myself in again settling to my profession. An event, however, occurred at this time, which threatened a diminution of my business, particularly among the society of which I was a member. This society had lately purchased in the city, a valuable piece of ground, for the purpose of erecting upon it a large meeting house, for Divine worship.[21] I was employed to prepare the deed of conveyance. I found everything regular, drew up the instrument, and, when it was engrossed, delivered it to the trustees, for their inspection before it was executed. When I expected the completion of this business, one of the trustees called upon me, and delicately observed, that in consequence of some doubt as to the validity of the instrument, they had applied to a lawyer of distinction and long established practice, who declared that the conveyance was void, being liable to the statutes of mortmain. I was greatly surprised and hurt; and clearly perceived, that if this opinion were not effectually counteracted, it would strike deeply at my reputation and practice as a lawyer. I therefore desired the person to leave the instrument with me, for a little time, when, I doubted not, I should be able to satisfy the trustees, that it was perfectly regular. I immediately laid the conveyance before the first counsellor in the province, and requested his opinion of it in writing. He gave it, in the most explicit language, and fully adapted to the case. It was, he said, in every respect, a good deed: and he observed, in particular, that none of the statutes of mortmain would affect it. My mind was completely relieved by this decision. I produced the opinion to the trustees, who were perfectly satisfied with it; and appeared to be much pleased, that I had so happily extricated myself from the difficulty. The result of this affair was exactly the reverse of what might at first have been expected. It established my reputation among the members of the society. My business increased; and they applied to me with confidence.

In the practice of the law, pecuniary interest was not my only rule of action. When circumstances would properly admit of it, I generally endeavoured to persuade the person who was threatened with a prosecution to pay the debt, or make satisfaction, without the trouble and expense of a suit. In doubtful cases, I frequently recommended a settlement of differences, by arbitration, as the mode which I conceived would ultimately prove most satisfactory to both parties. I do not recollect that I ever encouraged a client to proceed at law, when I thought his cause was unjust or indefensible: but, in such cases, I believe it was my invariable practice to discourage litigation, and to recommend a peaceful settlement of differences. . .

My business was very successful, and continued to increase till the troubles in America commenced.[22] A general failure of proceedings in the courts of law, then took place. This circumstance, joined to a severe illness, which had left me in a feeble state of health, induced me to remove into the country. We chose for our retreat a situation on Long Island, in the district of Islip,[23] about forty miles from the city of New York. Here we concluded to remain, till the political storm should blow over, and the horizon become again clear and settled. This we did not expect would be very soon; and therefore made our settlement accordingly. As our place of residence was on the borders of a large bay near the ocean, I purchased a very convenient, little pleasure-boat; which I thought would not only amuse me, but contribute to the reestablishment of my health. In this situation, I became extremely attached to the pleasures of shooting, and fishing, and sailing on the bay. These exercises probably gained for me an accession of health and strength; and, on that ground, partly reconciled me to an occupation of my time, which was but little connected with mental improvement. I have, however, often regretted that so long a period should have elapsed, without any vigorous application to study; and without an improved preparation for the return of those settled times, when I should again derive my support from the funds of knowledge and judgment. . .

But occupied as I was with amusement, my mind was not so much attached to it, as to be totally inattentive to every thing of a useful nature. About a year after my residence at Islip, the country became greatly distressed from the scarcity of salt. The British cruisers effectually prevented the introduction of that article among the Americans. And the Congress found it necessary to recommend and encourage the making of it, in every place that was favourably situated for the manufacture. I conceived that salt works might be advantageously erected on an island in the bay near which I resided; and I communicated this idea to an ingenious and spirited young man who was my neighbour. He very readily came into the plan, and joined me in the execution of it. We embraced the scheme the more cordially, because we were attached to our country, and felt for the distresses in which it was involved. We procured materials at a considerable expense, employed artificers to construct the works, and were just ready to begin the manufacture, and reap the fruit of our labours, when the British forces took possession of New York, and consequently of Long Island. This event entirely superseded our operations; as the article of salt was then abundantly introduced into the country. Our loss was considerable: but we had no remedy; and the whole concern was, therefore, without hesitation abandoned. . .

After we had resided at Islip about four years, I became dissatisfied with a mode of life, which consisted chiefly in amusement and bodily exercise. I perceived the necessity of doing something that would provide permanent funds for the expenses of my family.[24] The British power was still maintained at New York, and appeared likely to be established there: and the practice of the law was completely superseded. I had, therefore, no prospect of any considerable employment, but by settling at New York, and entering into mercantile concerns. We removed accordingly to the city, and took a situation favourable for business. My father very generously gave me an unlimited credit, in the importation of merchandise from London: and after forming the best judgment I could of the articles likely to be in demand, I made out a large order. The goods arrived, and I found a ready sale for them. Thus encouraged, I continued to import more of them, and that extensively every season; and soon perceived that I had engaged in a very lucrative occupation. Every year added to my capital, till, about the period of the establishment of American independence, I found myself able to gratify our favourite wishes, and retire from business.

I purchased a country seat on the banks of the river, about three miles from the city of New York. Here we promised ourselves every enjoyment that our hearts desired. Bellevue, for that was the name of our retreat, was most delightfully situated. A noble river, a mile in breadth, spread itself before us: a rich and pleasant country was on the opposite shore: and our view extended several miles both up and down the river. On this grand expanse of water, vessels and boats of various descriptions, were almost continually sailing. The house was neat and commodious; and accommodated with a spacious and elegant piazza, sashed with Venetian blinds; which added to its coolness in summer, and produced a most soothing and grateful effect. At the back of the mansion, was a large garden, well supplied with fruit, flowers, and useful vegetables: and in other directions from the house, were rows of various kinds of fruit trees, distinguished by their beauty and utility. In the rear of the house and garden, was a pleasant and fertile field, which afforded pasturage for the cattle. This little paradisiacal spot was perfectly to our wishes. Here we fondly hoped often to see our dearest connexions, and to entertain our friends. Every comfort to be derived from useful and interesting society, would, we imagined, be heightened in this pleasing abode. I thought too, that this retreat would be friendly to study and mental acquisitions; that my health would be improved, by the exercise which I should have in rural occupations; and that the vicinity of the city and its various institutions, would afford me opportunities of being useful to my fellow-citizens. These hopes and views appeared to be rational and well founded; and I felt no reluctance or compunction, in indulging them. But the pleasant prospects were soon overcast: the cup of promised sweets was not allowed to approach our lips. Divine Providence had allotted for us a different situation, and I have no doubt that the allotment was both wise and good; and better for us than our own fond appointments.

Before we removed to Bellevue, I had a severe fit of illness,[25] which left me in a very infirm and debilitated state of body. The tone of my muscles was so much impaired, that I could walk but little; and this relaxation continued to increase. I was besides, in the course of the day, frequently affected with singular sensations of chilness, succeeded by a degree of fever. My situation, at times, became very distressing. I was, however, encouraged by the hope, that a short residence at our delightful retreat, would restore me to my usual state of health and strength. But season succeeded season, without my receiving any salutary effect. I evidently grew worse: and my friends became alarmed at my situation. They generally recommended travelling. Additional exercise, new scenes, and drinking the waters of certain medicinal springs, were thought likely to afford me assistance. As my spirits were good, and life and health very desirable, I cordially entered into the views of my friends, and, with my affectionate and sympathizing partner, I set off for Bristol[26] in Pennsylvania. We remained in this rural and pleasant town a few weeks: during which time, I bathed, and drank the water; but without any good effect. The weather then growing extremely hot, Farenheit's thermometer being at ninety degrees, we proceeded to some celebrated springs in the mountains of New Jersey. Here, I seemed to grow better for a few weeks: but the water yielded no permanent benefit. From the very elevated situation of those mountains, the air was cool and refreshing: but as the roads were stony and broken, I could not have the advantage of regular exercise in a carriage. To remedy this inconvenience, I made some efforts on horseback, and some on foot: but these efforts fatigued me to a great degree, and increased the debility under which I laboured.

Perceiving that neither the springs, nor the situation, produced any beneficial effects, and travelling being one of the means for the recovery of health, which had been recommended to me, we left the mountains, and bent our course towards Bethlehem,[27] in Pennsylvania, a healthful and pleasant town about fifty miles from Philadelphia. This is a settlement of the Moravians. The situation of the place, its refreshing and salutary air, joined to the character of its inhabitants, made a cheering impression upon us; and we took up our quarters at the inn with pleasure, and with the hope of advantage. A few days after we had settled here, we were most agreeably surprised by the arrival of my father, and my sister Beulah. This affectionate parent had long been anxious about my health, and solicitous to promote it. And perceiving that we were not likely to return very soon, and that I had not received much benefit, he was desirous of spending a little time with us; which he naturally thought would have a cheering effect on his children, in their present solitary excursion. This visit was as grateful as it was unexpected. My sister was a sensible and amiable young woman, of a gentle nature and engaging manners, to whom we were both very nearly attached: we therefore formed a little band, closely united by the ties of affection and consanguinity. This pleasing association, joined to the beauty and retirement of the place, gave an animating impulse to my spirits; so that I was better at Bethlehem than I had been in any other part of the journey. . .[28]

The roads and scenery about Bethlehem were very delightful. I frequently enjoyed the pleasure they afforded, by riding in a small open carriage, which gave me a good opportunity of surveying the beauties of the country. In one of these excursions, I observed a gate which opened into some grounds that were very picturesque. Without proper consideration, I desired the servant who accompanied me, to open the gate. Almost immediately I observed a group of cheerful, neatly dressed young females approaching. They had been gathering blackberries, a rich fruit in that country; and each of them had a little basket in her hand filled with this sort of fruit. I soon perceived that I had committed a trespass, in offering to enter the grounds appropriated entirely to the walks of females. When they came near me, I apologised for the intrusion, by alleging that I did not know the peculiar use to which the enclosure was applied. With great good nature, and genuine politeness, some of them intimated that I was perfectly excusable. I believe the number of this cheerful group was about thirty, between the ages of fifteen and twenty-five. The sight of so much apparent innocence and happiness was extremely pleasing. And whilst they stood near the carriage, from which I could not conveniently alight, I thought it would be proper to express my respect and good wishes for them. I therefore took the liberty of addressing them in a short speech; which, as near as I can recollect, was to the following purport. I observed that it gave me particular pleasure, to see them all so happy: that their situation was, indeed, enviable, and singularly adapted to produce much real enjoyment, and to protect them from the follies, the vices, and the miseries, of the world: that if they knew the troubles and exposures, which are to be met with in the general intercourse of life, they would doubly enjoy their safe and tranquil seclusion from those dangers, and be thankful for the privileges they possessed. My harangue seemed to have a good effect upon them. They smiled, and some of them said that they were indeed happy in their situation. A few of them then held up their little baskets, and desired I would help myself to some fruit. I thanked them and took more than I wanted, that I might the better gratify their benevolence. I then parted with this pleasing company, and pursued another road, well satisfied with a mistake and adventure which had yielded me so much heart-felt satisfaction.

I must not omit to mention, that these good young persons reported to their superiors the whole of this transaction, with what had been said on the occasion. But I found that, notwithstanding my intrusion, I had lost no credit with the elderesses. For they sent to inform the sick gentleman, (this was the term by which I was designated,) that he had full liberty, and was welcome, whenever he chose, to ride in the grounds appropriated to the walks of the females. I acknowledged the favour of so great a privilege; but as I could not think it entirely warrantable and proper to make use of it, I never repeated my visit to this interesting place. . .

Having formed some acquaintance with several worthy persons in this happy town, and being much gratified with our visit, we took our leave with regret. I cannot easily forget the pleasing impressions which this settlement left upon my mind. The grandeur of the neighbouring hills; the winding course of its adjacent beautiful river; and the serene, enlivening state of the atmosphere; joined to the modest and tranquil appearance of the inhabitants; their frequent and devout performance of Divine worship; and their unaffected politeness and good humour; are sufficient to render Bethlehem a most interesting and delightful retreat. . .

After we left Bethlehem, where we had spent several weeks, it seemed expedient to bend our course towards home. My father was affected with fresh symptoms of a disorder to which he had long been subject; and he thought it would not be prudent to continue his visit any longer. Under these circumstances, we could not suffer him and my sister to proceed on their journey alone. Had he been as well as usual, it would have been very agreeable to us to have remained longer at Bethlehem; and particularly to have visited the place of my nativity, which was about fifty miles further in the interior of the country. This visit we had all contemplated; and purposed to set off for the place in a few days. But my father's sudden indisposition made it necessary to relinquish our views entirely. . . We proceeded, by easy stages, towards New York. There we safely arrived, after an agreeable journey; in which my father's health had not materially suffered, by the fatigue and exposure which he encountered, and which to him were unusual. . .

When we were again settled at Bellevue, we had rather mournfully to reflect on the little benefit, if any, which my health had derived from our summer excursion; and we naturally turned our attention to other means of relief that might promise success. During the course of my indisposition, I had found that I was generally better when the weather was cold: a temporary bracing was commonly the effect of the winter season. But we had observed that every succeeding summer took from me more than the winter had given. The prospect was therefore discouraging. Under these circumstances, I consulted one of the first physicians of the country, who happened at that time to be in New York. He paid a friendly attention to my situation; and after maturely considering the case, advised me to remove to a climate, where the summers are more temperate and less relaxing; and where, consequently, I might not lose, in warm weather, the bracing effects produced by the rigours of winter. From what he knew of Yorkshire, in England, he thought some parts of it might prove a proper situation. He thought that my disorder was of such a nature, that medicines would not be proper for me: 'at any rate', he said, 'I would advise you not to take much medicine.' This advice was consonant with the views and practice which I had long adopted: and confirmed me in my determination. For more than twenty years, I have almost entirely declined the use of medicines: and to this I attribute, in a great measure, the good appetite, and unbroken rest at nights, which, during that period, I have generally enjoyed. The natural tone of my stomach has not been injured by the operation of drugs, nor any new disorder superinduced. . .

After deliberately considering the advice of my physician, and the importance of the undertaking, we were fully convinced that it was expedient to try the effect of a more favourable climate, and to make a short residence in England. Dear as were our relatives and friends, and our native land, we resolved to forego the enjoyment of them. But hope cheered us with the prospect, that the separation would not be long; and that we should return to them, with renewed health and spirits, and capacities of greater happiness in their society. My dear wife did not hesitate a moment, in resolving to accompany me to a distant country; and to render me every aid, which her affection, and solicitude for my happiness, could suggest.

Soon after our determination was made, we prepared for the voyage. The trying scene now commenced of taking leave of our relations and friends. Many of them accompanied us to the ship, in the cabin of which we had a most solemn parting. An eminent minister[29] was present at this time, for whom we had a particular esteem and regard, and who prayed fervently on the occasion. It was a deeply affecting time; and, I trust, produced salutary impressions on all our minds. . . With many, if not with all, of those beloved connexions, we parted never to see them again, in this life: for many of them have since been translated to the world of spirits. But we humbly trust, that the separation will not be perpetual; that, through redeeming mercy and love, we shall be again united to virtuous connexions, and happily join with them, and the blessed of all generations, in glorifying our heavenly Father, and joyfully serving him for ever, with enlarged minds and purified affections.

We embarked in a commodious ship, near the close of the year 1784; and, after a prosperous voyage of about five-weeks, landed at Lymington. Near the conclusion of the voyage, we narrowly escaped some very dangerous rocks, which would, in all probability, have proved fatal to us, if we had struck upon them. Thus preserved by the care of a gracious Providence, we had fresh cause to be humbly thankful to God, and to be encouraged to trust in his goodness, for future preservation and direction.

In contemplating the place where we were to reside, during our continuance in England, it was our frequent and special desire, that our lot might be cast in the neighbourhood and society of religious and exemplary persons; from whom we might derive encouragement to the practice of virtue. We had lived long enough to perceive, how strongly the human mind is influenced, and how apt it is to be moulded, by the dispositions and pursuits of those with whom it is intimately connected. We had felt the danger of intercourse with persons, who seemed to make the pleasures of this life the great object of their attention; and we had derived comfort, and some degree of religious strength, from the society and example of good and pious persons. . .

Our attachment to England was founded on many pleasing associations. In particular, I had strong prepossessions in favour of a residence in this country; because I was ever partial to its political constitution, and the mildness and wisdom of its general system of laws. I knew that, under this excellent government, life, property, reputation, civil and religious liberty are happily protected; and that the general character and virtue of its inhabitants, take their complexion from the nature of their constitution and laws. On leaving my native country, there was not, therefore, any land, on which I could cast my eyes with so much pleasure; nor is there any, which could have afforded me so much real satisfaction, as I have found in Great Britain. . .

In a few days after our landing, we reached London. Here we were cheered with the society of a number of our friends, whom we had known, in the visit which we made to this country in the year 1771. We continued in and near London, about six weeks; and then proceeded for Yorkshire. Some of our friends advised us to fix our residence at Pontefract, others at Knaresborough, and others at Richmond, Settle, or upon the Wolds. We, however, thought it prudent to visit a number of places, before we concluded to fix upon any one. At length, we came to York: and whether we were influenced by the association of names,[30] by the pleasantness of the surrounding country, or by other motives, we felt some partiality for the place. But it appeared to be difficult to procure a suitable residence in the vicinity: and we left York to visit Knaresborough, Harrogate, and the neighbourhood of Leeds. Soon after we had set off, we observed, about a mile from the city, in a small village called Holdgate, a house and garden very pleasantly and healthfully situated. The place struck our minds so agreeably, that we stopped the carriage, for a few minutes, to survey it. The more we observed the house and its appendages, the more we liked them; and we concluded that if they could be obtained, they would suit us better than any other we had seen. With this reflection, we passed on, and continued our journey. At Knaresborough and Harrogate, we stayed a short time: but neither of these places appeared to coincide with our views, and we went forward to Leeds. From this place, I wrote to a friend at York, and requested him to inquire, whether the house near that city, which had so pleasantly impressed us, could be either hired or purchased, and on what terms. My friend informed me, that the owner of this estate resided upon it, that he had considerably improved it, and that it was perfectly to his mind; so that he intended to occupy it for the remainder of his life. All prospect of acquiring this situation being thus cut off, we employed ourselves in looking at several other places near Leeds. But our attachment to York still continued, and after several weeks' absence from it, we returned, with the hope that some suitable place, in the neighbourhood of this city, would yet be found. That we might have the fairer opportunity for selecting such a residence, I hired for six months a house ready-furnished, in York; and occasionally made inquiry for a situation in its vicinity. About five months of the time elapsed before any place occurred which was adapted to our wishes. At this period, the house and premises which had appeared to us so desirable, were advertised for sale. The owner, who was an officer in the navy, had unexpectedly an offer made to him of a ship on a remote station; and being pleased with the appointment, he concluded to take his family with him, and to dispose of his property at Holdgate. I did not hesitate to apply as a purchaser; and, in a short time, the contract was made, and the estate secured to me.[31] We soon removed into our new residence; and found it to answer, in every respect, the expectations we had formed. It is healthy, pleasant, commodious, and unites the advantages of both town and country...

When I first settled at Holdgate, my general health had been, in some degree, improved; and I was able to walk in the garden, without assistance, several times in the course of a day. This increase of strength, and ability to walk out in the open air, were highly pleasing; and gave a fresh spring to our hopes, that the period was not very far distant, when we might return to our native country and our friends, with the blessings of established health, and all the comforts which follow in its train. But these cheering prospects did not long continue. The exercise in my garden was so delightful, and appeared to be so beneficial to me, that I often indulged myself in it; till, at length, I found my little stock of newly acquired strength, began to decline, and that the former weakness of the muscles returned. This was not the effect of great and immoderate exertion; but proceeded from my not knowing how very limited my bodily powers were, and from not keeping within those limits. I soon perceived that it was necessary to give up my little excursions in the garden: but I continued to walk occasionally about the room, as much as I was well able to bear, knowing the danger of resigning myself to a state of inactivity. This practice was kept up, in a greater or less degree, till it became inconvenient and painful. A walk even from my seat to the window, at last overcame me, and produced a distressing weariness and fatigue, which pervaded the whole animal system. I occasionally made repeated efforts to overcome these effects: but all to no purpose; the more I persisted in my exertions, the more painful was my situation. I perceived that I was always better, and more at my ease, when I continued sitting. This induced me to try the experiment of relinquishing all attempts at walking, and to keep to my seat through the course of the day. The result was, in every respect, beneficial. The soreness of the muscles abated; the little tone which remained in them, was not disturbed or overstretched; and I enjoyed an easy and tolerable state of health.

 I made it a point, however, to ride out daily in my carriage: and this, doubtless, contributed to counteract the injurious effects which would have resulted from constant inaction. The motion of the carriage, the change of scene, difference of air, and the busy or the cheerful faces of my fellow-creatures, produced a pleasing effect on my mind, and greatly tended to reconcile me to the privation of other exercises. Though I had not sufficient strength to get into a carriage, by the usual method, I have always been able to effect it, by means of a board laid nearly level from the garden gate to the step of the carriage. But I have repeatedly found this exertion to be the full extent of my powers. I can, however, generally accomplish it, with little or no inconvenience. This mode of getting into the carriage, has often excited the curiosity of persons who were passing at the time, and given rise to strange surmises, and to some ridiculous stories. . .

 The state of weakness and confinement to which I was now reduced, would, at some periods of my life, have been almost insupportable. But my infirmities had increased upon me gradually, and I had the happiness to perceive that they might be made to conduce to my future and immortal interests. I had many enjoyments and advantages yet left to me : I was, in general, free from pain; I could take a little daily exercise; my appetite was good; and my rest at nights commonly sound and uninterrupted. I had the society of worthy and intelligent friends, converse with books, and a regular correspondence with my distant connexions. I was able, too, to

Continuation of letter:

On the 27th Inst. I received a letter from thee, with several dates, viz. the 9th the 15th and the 19th of 12th mo: 1818, which contains the following communication.
" 12 mo 19- I have purchased for thee a share in the Bank of New York
" at 30 of 6th advance aims to $651$^{62}$/100 – and as we cannot always sell
" small Bills to suit, I have so arranged the business (having occasion
" to draw on Jn. Hadwin of Liverpool) as to the value on thee for £168 – St.
" which will include the cost of the Bank share, the £10 St. to be paid the
" widow Taylor, and £11.16 St. which I intend to request Isaac Hadwin
" to acct. to thee for, being the difference between £110 St. and the sum
" I drew on him for – this arrangement I presume will meet thy
" approbation – it seems that one half of the £110 St. is part of a Legacy
" which dear M. Routh bequeathed to the Nine Partners Boarding School.
   This communication I am unable to understand. How is it consistent with the drawing of the two aforementioned Bills upon me? Perhaps thou canst explain it. Possibly the purchase of these two Bills occured to thee afterwards, and the arrangements contained in this recited passage with respect to my concerns, was of course superseded.

*Letter from Lindley Murray 30th of 1st month 1819 to his brother John in New York regarding finance.*

attend public religious worship, once or twice in the week,[32] which I consider as an invaluable privilege. There still remained to me the great blessing of an affectionate, faithful friend, my beloved wife; whose solicitude to promote my comfort, in all respects, has been lively and uniform, through every period of our union. . .

In the summer of 1786, I met with a great loss, in the decease of my father. He had been painfully affected, with a cough and weakness of the stomach, for more than thirty years; and the disorder at length increased so much, that nature could no longer support the conflict. . . Thus peacefully left the world my dear and affectionate father, in the sixty-fifth year of his age; and, I trust, exchanged this life for one infinitely better.

After I left America, my father, during the remainder of his life, kindly transacted all my business; and obliged me with a regular correspondence, from which I derived much comfort and satisfaction. The religious state of mind which his letters demonstrated, under the pressure of years and infirmities, afforded me peculiar pleasure at the time; and continues to be a source of grateful recollection. The loss which I had sustained, in being deprived of my father's kind offices, my truly valuable brother, John Murray,[33] was studious to repair. For more than twenty years, he has attended to my concerns in America; and maintained a correspondence with me, in the most brotherly and affectionate manner. . . We were affectionately attached to each other, in early life: this attachment has not only continued, but it has increased with time; and I firmly trust it will remain, and brighten to the latest period of our lives. From my dear sisters, I have also received, in this long absence, many testimonies of their sincere regard, and solicitude for my welfare. These could not fail of being soothing to us; and they tended to cherish the feelings of mutual affection. . .

When I became confined, and incapable of but very little bodily exercise, I was not wholly deprived of every species of exertion. I could still employ myself in reading, in writing, and in conversation. My mind was preserved free and active. I might therefore hope to be exercised in doing something that would be useful to myself and others: something that would agreeably employ my mental powers; and prevent that tedium and irritability, which bodily infirmities too often occasion. This might be accomplished in various ways; and I ventured to believe it might, in part, be effected by a publication which I had in view, and which I presumed would be interesting to many readers. In the early part of my life, as well as in its succeeding periods, I had a lively pleasure and satisfaction, in perusing the sentiments of eminent and virtuous persons, on the subject of religion and futurity, when they approached the close of life.[34] From men[35] who had known the world, and who were qualified, and disposed, to give a true estimate of its nature and enjoyments, and whom we could not suspect of dissimulation at that awful period, much important instruction, I conceived, might be derived; and I trust I have been, in some degree, benefited by studies of this kind. . . Under these impressions, or views of the subject, I commenced my little work. As I wished to form it on liberal principles, and render it acceptable to readers in general, I was careful to introduce characters of various religious professions, and of different ages and countries. The concurrence of these, in the recommendation of religion, as the great promoter of our happiness here and hereafter, would, I conceived, form a strong persuasive evidence, in the cause of piety and virtue. . .

The first edition of this book, which was entitled, 'The Power of Religion on the Mind, etc.,' appeared in the year 1787. It consisted of only five hundred copies; all of which were neatly bound, and distributed at my own expense. I sent them to the principal inhabitants of York and its vicinity; and accompanied each book with an anonymous note requesting a favourable acceptance of it, and apologizing for the liberty I had taken. It was not without some hesitation, that I adopted so singular a mode of distribution. But, on mature reflection, I believed it to be more eligible than any other, for the purpose which I had in view. . .

I soon found that my publication was well received: and it was not long before I was encouraged to print a new edition of the work, in London, which met with a good sale. Several other impressions appeared in different places. When, after some time, a sixth edition was called for, I was induced to enlarge the book, and to put my name to it. And as I afterwards found that it continued to make a favourable progress, I conceived that if the copyright were assigned to some booksellers of extensive business and influence, it would be circulated more diffusively, and my design in composing it be still more effectually answered. Under this idea, I extended the work considerably; made some improvements in the language; and then disposed of the copyright,[36] without any pecuniary recompense. With this plan, I have every reason to be perfectly satisfied. The demand for the book has far exceeded my utmost expectations: and the testimonies of approbation, and of its usefulness, which I have received, have been truly gratifying. . .

At the close of the year 1794, I was seized with a severe illness, which continued for many weeks; and reduced me to so feeble a state, that my recovery was much doubted. During the continuance of this affliction, I was often desirous, that, if it were the will of Divine Providence, I might be removed from this state of trouble, and landed safely, as I hoped through infinite mercy I should be, on those happy shores, where there is neither sickness nor sorrow. . .

I was often solicited to compose and publish a Grammar of the English language, for the use of some teachers, who were not perfectly satisfied with any of the existing grammars.[37] I declined, for a considerable time, complying with this request, from a consciousness of my inability to do the subject that justice, which would be expected in a new publication of this nature. But being much pressed to undertake the work, I, at length turned my attention seriously to it. I conceived that a grammar containing a careful selection of the most useful matter, and an adaptation of it to the understanding, and the gradual progress of learners, with a special regard to the propriety and purity of all the examples and illustrations; would be some improvement on the English grammars which had fallen under my notice. With this impression, I ventured to produce the first edition of a work on this subject. It appeared in the spring of the year 1795.[38] I will not assert, that I have accomplished all that I proposed. But the approbation[39] and the sale which the book obtained, have given me some reason to believe, that I have not altogether failed in my endeavours to elucidate the subject, and to facilitate the labours of both teachers and learners of English grammar.

In a short time after the appearance of the work, a second edition was called for. This unexpected demand, induced me to revise and enlarge the book. It soon obtained an extensive circulation. And the repeated editions through which it passed in a few years, encouraged me, at length, to improve and extend it still further; and, in particular, to support, by some critical discussions, the principles upon which many of its positions are founded.

Soon after the Grammar had been published, I was persuaded to compose a volume of Exercises, calculated to correspond with, and illustrate, by copious examples, all the rules of the Grammar, both principal and subordinate. At the same time, I formed a Key to the Exercises, designed for the convenience of teachers, and for the use of young persons, who had left school, and who might be desirous, at their leisure, to improve themselves in grammatical studies and perspicuous[40] composition. In forming these two latter volumes, my design was, not only to exercise the student's ingenuity, in correcting the sentences; and to excite him to the study of grammar, by the pleasure of feeling his own powers and progress: but to introduce, for his imitation, a great number of sentences, selected from the best writers, and distinguished by their perspicuity and elegance; and to imbue his mind with sentiments of the

# ENGLISH GRAMMAR,

*ADAPTED TO THE DIFFERENT CLASSES OF*

LEARNERS.

WITH AN

APPENDIX,

CONTAINING

RULES AND OBSERVATIONS FOR PROMOTING PERSPICUITY
IN SPEAKING AND WRITING.

By L. MURRAY.

YORK:

PRINTED AND SOLD BY WILSON, SPENCE, AND MAWMAN.

1795.

*Title page of the First Edition of the English Grammar 1795.*

highest importance, by interweaving principles of piety and virtue with the study of language. The Exercises and Key were published in 1797; and met with a greater sale than I could have supposed. The approbation they received made ample amends to me, for the time and labour I had bestowed upon them. And I was encouraged, in the same year, to make an Abridgement of the Grammar, for the use of minor schools, and for those who were beginning to study the language. The four volumes being intimately connected, mutually supported and recommended each other. And this circumstance, I believe, induced many teachers to adopt them, in their seminaries of education.

As these books, except the Abridgement, were reprinted at York,[41] I consented to correct the press; by which, I presume, they appeared with a greater degree of accuracy, (a point of considerable importance to books designed for schools,) than if they had not received the author's inspection. This circumstance contributed to occupy some of my leisure hours; and, for a time, afforded a little amusement. Inconvenient as the employment afterwards proved, when it increased much beyond my expectation, I still continued it, with a hope that it would be productive of good effects. My examination of the new editions, gave occasion to many corrections and considerable enlargements; which I flatter myself, have improved the books, and rendered them less unworthy of the extensive patronage they have received.

In the course of my literary labours, I found that the mental exercise which accompanied them, was not a little beneficial to my health. The motives which excited me to write, and the objects which I hoped to accomplish, were of a nature calculated to cheer the mind, and to give the animal spirits a salutary impulse. I am persuaded, that if I had suffered my time to pass away, with little or no employment, my health would have been still more impaired, my spirits depressed, and perhaps my life considerably shortened. . .

These considerations, joined to the unexpected success which I had met with in my publications, encouraged me to persevere in my literary pursuits. I engaged in a work, which appeared to me likely to prove of peculiar advantage to the rising generation. This was a compilation containing some of the most esteemed pieces in the language, both in prose and poetry: which are at once calculated to promote correct reading; to give a taste for justness of thought, and elegance of composition; and to inculcate pious and virtuous sentiments. This work I entitled, 'The English Reader': and I was pleased to find that my hopes respecting it, were not disappointed. My book was introduced, as I wished it to be, into many schools and private families; and it has often been reprinted.

The approbation given to the English Reader, induced me to publish an 'Introduction' and a 'Sequel' to that book. These three volumes pursue the same subjects; they all aim at a chaste and guarded education of young persons. And I have great satisfaction in reflecting, that whilst they contain many selections which present the moral virtues, religion, and the Christian religion in particular, in very amiable points of view, not a sentiment has been admitted into any of them, which can pain the most virtuous mind, or give the least offence to the eye or ear of modesty.[42]

The recommendations which these books received, for the chastity and correctness of sentiment, which distinguish the pieces they contain, persuaded me to believe, that a collection, in French, on similar principles, and made from some of the finest writers; would be received by the public, with some degree of approbation. Animated by this expectation, I produced in the year 1802, a compilation entitled, 'Lecteur François', and in 1807, another, with the title of 'Introduction au Lecteur François'. As the contents of both these volumes are extracted from authors of reputation, and particularly guarded in point of sentiment and morality, I hoped that they would be acceptable to teachers of schools, and private instructers [sic], as well as to the young persons who were under their care, and others who wished to improve themselves in the language. . .

In the year 1804, I published a Spelling Book. When it first occurred to me to compose this little book, and for some time afterwards, the work appeared to be of so very humble a nature, that I was not in much haste to set about it. On reflecting, however, that a Spelling book is commonly the threshold of learning; and that, by introducing into it a number of easy reading lessons, calculated to attract attention, the infant mind might be imbued with the love of goodness, and led to approve and practice many duties connected with early life; my hesitation was removed, and, after a considerable time, the work was completed. But I found it much more difficult than I expected. The adaptation of lessons to the young capacity, and the exactness required in the gradations of instruction, appeared to demand all the judgment and attention of which I was master; and probably called for much more than I possessed. After many essays, I came at length to the end of my labour. I made it a point, in composing the Spelling book, to introduce no matter that is foreign to the objects which such a work ought to have in view; and I was studious to bring the latter reading lessons to such a state of advancement, as would form an easy and natural connexion between this book and the 'Introduction to the English Reader.'

From the friend whom I am now addressing, and at whose request these Memoirs are written,[43] I certainly received much valuable, and very material assistance, in compiling the Spelling Book, The Introduction to the English Reader, and the two volumes in French: and I cannot, with propriety, omit, on the present occasion, the acknowledgement of this co-operation. It is also proper to add, in this place, that I received from the same hand, and from a number of my literary correspondents, many useful suggestions and criticisms, with respect to my English Grammar, and some of my other publications. Those hints and criticisms have undoubtedly contributed, in no small degree, to improve the books, and to render them less unworthy of the attention which they have received from the public.

As I was desirous that my publications should have a circulation as extensive as I could procure for them, I sold the copyrights to one of the first houses in London.[44] These booksellers had it in their power to spread them very diffusively; and they have done it perfectly to my satisfaction. They gave a liberal price for the books: and I must say, that in all our transactions together, which have not been very limited, they have demonstrated great honour and uprightness, and entirely justified my confidence and expectations. I have great pleasure in knowing that the purchase of the copyrights has proved highly advantageous to them: and though it has turned out much more lucrative, than was at first contemplated, they are fully entitled to the benefit. Such contracts have always in them some degree of hazard; and it was possible that these might have been attended with little or no profit.

But my views in writing and publishing were not of a pecuniary nature. My great objects were, as I before observed, to be instrumental in doing a little good to others, to youth in particular; and to give my mind a rational and salutary employment. It was, I believe, my early determination, that if any profits should arise from my literary labours, I would apply them, not to my own private use, but to charitable purposes, and for the benefit of others.[45] My income was sufficient to support the expenses of my family,[46] and to allow of a little to spare; and I had not any children to provide for. . .

After the Grammar and the books connected with it, had passed through many editions, the proprietors conceived that an edition of the whole, in two volumes octavo, on fine paper, and in a large letter, would be well received by the public; and I embraced the opportunity, to improve the work, by many additions which I conceived to be appropriate. These occupied about one hundred pages of the first volume. In its present form, the publication is designed for the use of persons who may think it merits a place in their libraries. To this privilege it may, perhaps, be allowed to aspire, as a work containing a pretty extensive

AN

# ENGLISH GRAMMAR:

COMPREHENDING

THE PRINCIPLES AND RULES

OF THE

*LANGUAGE,*

ILLUSTRATED BY

APPROPRIATE EXERCISES,

AND

A KEY TO THE EXERCISES.

---

BY *LINDLEY MURRAY.*

---

They who are learning to compose and arrange their sentences with accuracy and order, are learning, at the same time, to think with accuracy and order. ................ BLAIR.

---

IN TWO VOLUMES.

---

VOLUME I.

---

*A NEW EDITION.*

---

**York:**

Printed by Thomas Wilson & Son, High-Ousegate,

FOR LONGMAN, HURST, REES, AND ORME ; AND DARTON AND HARVEY, LONDON:
FOR WILSON AND SON, AND R. AND W. SPENCE, YORK : AND
FOR CONSTABLE AND CO. EDINBURGH.

1808.

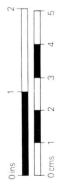

*Title page of 1808 Grammar.*

32

exhibition of the principles of English grammar, and a copious illustration of those principles; with the addition of some positions and discussions, which I persuade myself are not destitute of originality. It will, therefore, I venture to hope, serve as a book of reference, to refresh the memory, and, in some degree, to employ the curiosity of persons who are skilled in grammar, as well as to extend the knowledge of those who wish to improve themselves in the art. This octavo edition of the Grammar appeared in 1808. It was favourably received; and a new edition of it was ordered in the course of a few months.

At this period, I had the satisfaction to perceive, that all my literary productions were approved; and that most of them were advancing in the public estimation. But I was fully persuaded, that an author ought to terminate his labours, before the tide of favour begins to turn; and before he incurs the charge of being so infected with the morbid humour for writing, as not to have the discretion to know when to stop. I was so sensible of what was due to the public, for their favourable reception of my productions, that I was extremely unwilling to forfeit their approbation, by presuming too much on what I had experienced. . . I may add to these observations, that I had, perhaps, pursued this mode of employment rather too closely; and that I wished for more leisure to prosecute other studies. Influenced by these various motives, I have closed my literary labours, for the present at least; and I shall not resume them, unless some special considerations should alter my views of the subject. There will, I trust, still remain for me, other sources of employment, and some degree of usefulness, better adapted to circumstances, and to my growing infirmities of body. . .

At the close of the year 1808, I met with a most affecting event, in the death of my youngest sister, the wife of Gilbert Colden Willett.[47] She had been, for nearly a year, much indisposed; and the disorder made a gradual progress, till it put a period to her mortal existence, in the forty-fifth year of her age. From the letters of my relations which mention her decease, and the circumstances attending it, I have derived great consolation. She was so patient, so fully resigned to the will of God, and so well prepared to leave the world, and enter into a state of blessedness; that we have no cause to mourn on her account. She has, doubtless, commenced that life, which is free from temptation and sorrow; and in which she will be unspeakably happy for ever. I rejoice that I have had such a sister; and I trust that the recollection of her pious and bright example, will prove, through life, a source of thankfulness, and an additional incentive to virtue. . .

I cannot finish these Memoirs of my life, without expressing, still more particularly, my sense of the greatest blessing which was ever conferred on mankind. I mean,· the redemption from sin, and the attainment of a happy immortality, by the atonement and intercession of our Lord and Saviour, Jesus Christ. I contemplate this wonderful proof of the love of God to man, as an act of mercy and benignity, which will stimulate the gratitude and love, the obedience, praise, and adoration, of the redeemed, through ages that will never end. . .

*Notes* *Chapter I*

[1] About 50 miles West of Philadelphia.
[2] Robert Murray, 1721-1786; he emigrated from Scotland in 1732 and became one of the most successful merchants in New York. He was an active Friend.
[3] L.M. often used colons and semicolons where we would use commas.
[4] Mary Murray, born Lindley. According to John F. Mines in an article in Scribner's (1876) she was 'a celebrated Quaker belle'; she enabled the American General Putnam to make his escape from New York in 1776 by inviting the pursuing British commander, Lord Howe, to dinner at the Murray home. The pleasure-loving general could not refuse the welcome of the fair Quaker and her beautiful daughters. Mary Murray's assistance to the Republican cause has been recognised by the Knickerbocker Chapter of the Daughters of the American Revolution, which has erected a monument to her in Manhattan at Park Avenue and 37th Street. It appears that Robert Murray approved of loyalty to the Crown – he signed a petition of welcome to the British, but his wife and daughters were ardent republicans, according to this late surmise. He, and his son Lindley also, were among the 17 Friends who signed the protest from New York Meeting at the British commanders' orders that they patrol the streets in the city watch: 'they could not in conscience support or contribute directly or indirectly to the practice or business of war'.
[5] A precocious child! Elizabeth Frank states that he showed no promise as a baby 'either of bodily or mental vigour'. His perpetual crying depressed his mother, who often said it would have been a mercy both to the child and his parents if he had not survived.
[6] i.e. unruly.
[7] i.e. outcome.
[8] L.M.'s memory is here at fault. His name appears in the school enrolment list for 1756 when he was 11 or 12. His teacher, Ebenezer Kinnersley, did not join the staff till 1754. The school owed its inspiration to Benjamin Franklin, who was keen that the English language should be taught by grammar.

Kinnersley had collaborated with Franklin in some of his early experiments in electricity.

[9] The year was 1757 or 8.

[10] Elizabeth Frank records that 'in early life he was fond of shooting; but after some years he became dissatisfied with it, from a conviction, not only that it consumes too much precious time, but also that it is improper to take away life for the sake of amusement. He believed that of the birds which are shot at, many more are wounded, than are actually killed, and consequently they die through pain and want of food. He determined never again to indulge himself in a sport which produced so much distress to the objects of his amusement'.

[11] Robert Murray obtained a certificate from his Monthly Meeting to Philadelphia Monthly Meeting on Lindley's going to Philadelphia as an apprentice, 3.12.1761. Friends normally carried such certificates of introduction when moving to another Monthly Meeting area.

[12] i.e. proceeds.

[13] i.e. pleasure.

[14] NE of Philadelphia on the New Jersey side of the Delaware.

[15] See the list of past participles in the Grammar, which gives *rid* in 1799, but *rode* or *ridden* in 1804, with a note that *ridden* is nearly obsolete.

[16] i.e. lack of religious faith.

[17] 1775.

[18] Hannah Dobson.

[19] June 22, 1767. The marriage was not according to Friends Discipline, but the Monthly Meeting held at Flushing on 3.9.1767 accepted the following apology from Lindley:

'After having seriously reflected upon the Subject of marriage, I can with Truth and Sincerity say that I am very sorry to have acted in this Matter contrary to the Discipline of Friends, and without the approbation of my Parents: that I condemn it as being performed by a Priest: and upon the Whole I am sensibly concerned for every Violation of the Good Rules and order of your Society. . . I therefore earnestly ask for the Continuance of your Care and Regard, which I will endeavour by my Future Conduct to merit and retain
          Your respectful Friend:
          Lindley Murray'

[20] John, Beulah and Susannah. Their certificate for travel was presented to Devonshire House Monthly Meeting, 5.2.1771.

[21] New York Preparative Meeting first asked permission to buy land for the Pearl St. Meeting House in 1771; subscriptions were collected in 1774 (Robert Murray giving £100 and Lindley £20) and work began under a committee which included Robert Murray, recently returned from England. The large brick meeting house was completed in 1776. Robert Murray left £200 for a room to be added for women's meetings.

[22] The American War of Independence began in 1775 and ended in 1783.

[23] On a bay on the South shore of Long Island.

[24] i.e. household. L.M. had no children.
[25] The symptoms he describes suggest he had a rare endocrine or a muscular disorder.
[26] Across the Delaware from Burlington, about 20 miles NE of Philadelphia.
[27] North of Philadelphia, near the Delaware.
[28] A digression follows on the Moravian custom of having marriages arranged by their 'elders and elderesses'.
[29] Probably a Recorded Minister of the Society of Friends.
[30] i.e. with New York.
[31] William Tuke bought the house on behalf of the Murrays, and paid a fine of £33 to Acomb Manor Court (9.11.85) for renewal of the copyhold, and later £11/5/0 for the addition to the property of two closes. The builder had acquired the site in 1770. Geo. Dawson RN bought the house in 1783 and sold it to William Tuke on receiving the command of the frigate *Phaeton* in 1785. William Tuke left it in his will to his son John and his grandson Samuel. Samuel Tuke's son, William Murray Tuke, lived there for 10 years before he moved to London in 1849. The Backhouse family moved there in 1859.
[32] Meetings for Worship were held in the Meeting House in Clifford St., twice on Sundays and also midweek. The large Meeting House had to be demolished in 1979 due to its foundations becoming unsafe. This left the small Meeting House for use for worship and new rooms were built in the place of the large Meeting House, the old Friargate entrance being reverted to for use as in L.M.'s time.
[33] John Murray was active in business and became President of the New York Chamber of Commerce. He was an active Friend; his marriage to Catharine Bowne in 1783 was a model of compliance with Friends usage. His home was a centre of Quaker work, e.g. women Friends met there to form a committee for charity relief for non-Quakers. Catharine Murray was treasurer to this work for 19 years. Men Friends likewise met in the Murray home in 1805 to found a school for boys in the city slums. With Lindley, John was on the first board of Trustees of Friends Seminary, founded by New York Monthly Meeting, with the encouragement of Yearly Meeting, in 1786. Robert Murray left the school £200. (See *Children of Light, Friends Seminary, 1786-1986,* by Nancy Reid Gibbs, published by the School.) Lindley had been clerk of the committee appointed by New York Preparative Meeting to superintend the school and reported appointing a schoolmaster and opening the school (26.5.84).
[34] cf. *The Annual Monitor,* founded and edited by Ann (Tuke) Alexander from 1813, which recorded the sayings of dying Friends as support to the living.
[35] The second edition added many examples of women.
[36] Probably to Darton & Harvey of 55 Gracechurch St., London.
[37] Ann and Mabel Tuke, who taught in the Trinity Lane school for Quaker girls, founded by Esther Tuke in 1784, and Martha Fletcher, who had gone from Trinity Lane to teach in Sarah (Tuke) Grubb's school at Suir Island, Clonmel, Ireland, They wrote:

'To the Rt. Honble. Lindley Murray, Teacher of the English Language & etc. & etc.

The humble petition of Ann Tuke, Mabel Tuke, and Martha Fletcher, showeth,

That they, and their Sister professors at Suir Island, having for a series of time, suffered great inconvenience from the want of a complete English Grammar, with examples and rules annexed, proper for this and similar Institutions; and their expectations of a timely supply from the Inspector of a neighbouring seminary, being rendered frustrate, by a conference with their honourable Father, who has no apprehension that such a production will be brought forward: and his petitioners being well assured of the incomparable abilities of their able preceptor, do humbly solicit the digesting of his materials for a work so important; in the execution of which they will gladly afford him their feeble assistance. And his Petitioners will, as in duty bound, desire (also pray) that his labours may be amply rewarded by the manifest fruits of its utility to the present and succeeding generations.

    Ann Tuke    Mabel Tuke    Martha Fletcher

L.M. replied: 'Lindley Murray entertains such a respect for his dear friends Ann Tuke, Mabel Tuke, and Martha Fletcher, that it would be no easy matter for him to refuse any request which they might think proper to make. With respect, however, to the present one he can but hesitate for two considerations. 1st. he fears he is not competent to compile a Grammar for publication, and if that were not a sufficient reason, he apprehends the London Committee have employed some person on this business who is now engaged upon it. But should this not appear to be the case on enquiry and if my little labours be confined to the schools of York and Clonmel, an extent abundantly sufficient for them, I purpose to make some essay to comply with your desires in which I shall be certain of at least one satisfaction, that of having endeavoured to please and accommodate those who have much of the love and esteem of their sincerely attached friend    Lindley Murray'.

N.B. The London Committee which L.M. mentions was probably the London Committee of Ackworth School (there was also a Country Committee of local Friends). Ackworth had a manual of its own, produced by school staff, and known from its publisher's name as Thomas Coar's Grammar (see Henry Thompson, *History of Ackworth School*, p.104). Murray's Grammar was introduced at Ackworth in 1805.

Sarah Grubb had died in 1790. L.M. compiled an Account of her Life and Religious Labours, with an Appendix on the Schools at Ackworth and York; it was published anonymously in Dublin in 1792.

[38] He had begun work in the spring of 1794.

[39] Elizabeth Frank quotes several complimentary reviews, e.g. 'His works are distinguished from the mass of school books by a correct style, a refined taste and especially by a vigilant subservience to morality and religion'. (*Eclectic Review*). The first edition was soon sold out, and a second was called for in 1796.

[40] i.e. clear.

[41] by Wilson & Sons.
[42] L.M. comments (Memoir p. 104) that several classical writers contain passages which might 'corrupt the tender minds of youth', and applauds the bowdlerised editions which had been published, though he thinks more remains to be done. E. Frank adds that he also felt that 'a purified edition of the British Poets' was needed.
[43] Elizabeth Frank. The Memoirs were written in the form of letters to her.
[44] Longmans. E. Frank gives the prices he received (Memoir pp. 261-2): Grammar, Exercises and Key – £700; Abridgement – £100; Reader – £350; Sequel – £200; Introduction – £200; Lecteur & Intro. – £700; Spelling Book and First Book for Children – £500.
[45] A minute of Trinity Lane School (26.3.1798) 'gratefully acknowledges the receipt of £100 from our friend Lindley Murray, being a donation from him to the institution arising from the sale of the Abridgement of his Grammar, which in addition to the advantage the school has derived from the sale of the Grammar, Exercises, etc. accounts for the gain of last year.' In 1799 he said that having sold the copyright of the Grammar and Exercises, he would use part of the money for the school, at £46 p.a. for about eight years.
[46] i.e. household. But he also helped his family in America.
[47] Mary. L.M. adds a detailed description of her last days, her faith in Christ and her religious consolation of her husband. She had been disowned by Friends for marrying out, 4.6.1796.

*LINDLEY MURRAY'S INVALID CHAIR*
*Given to The Mount School by the family of Tyndale Procter, who was Hon. Treasurer to the school 1912-37. (Note the wheels for ease of mobility.)*

CHAPTER II

# Elizabeth Frank's Account

ELIZABETH FRANK lived with the Murrays for a number of years as their companion, and then moved to a house of her own nearby on The Mount. She had first met Lindley Murray in 1793 and helped him in his work on his books (she published works in a similar genre herself[1]). It was she who encouraged him to write an account of his life, which he did in the form of a series of letters to her. These he finished in the spring of 1809, leaving it to her to complete the story and publish the whole in a Memoir after his death. She was appointed his literary executor, with instructions to destroy his unpublished letters and papers.

She describes him as a tall and well-proportioned man, with a dark complexion, regular features and a high and open forehead. Despite his illness he did not look sickly. An American visitor described his face as ruddy and animated, with a strong expression of benevolence. His manner of conversing, he said, was modest, gentle, easy and persuasive.

His physical condition deteriorated in 1809, so that he was no longer able to go out in his carriage or even spend time in his chair in the garden.[2] Even very limited exercise increased his muscular weakness, and he caught cold easily. He experimented with outings in a sedan chair, but felt they did him no good. In 1810 he had a severe illness culminating in the discharge of a small stone, and for several years after suffered from pain in head, stomach and bowels. He therefore spent the last 16 years of his life wholly confined to the house.

He was cared for by his faithful wife, Hannah, assisted in these later years by one servant and a companion, who read to them and helped Mrs. Murray with the house-keeping. We hear little of Hannah, but he always speaks of her with loving appreciation, and on her birthday, which was also their wedding anniversary, he would write her a note of thankfulness for their happy marriage. Elizabeth Frank says of her: 'Mrs. Murray is not a showy woman, nor particularly literary, but she possesses a solid understanding, great firmness of mind and a particularly kind disposition. To the poor and afflicted, she is, in a high degree, liberal and compassionate. By her skill and prudence in the management of her household affairs she relieved her husband of all anxiety on these subjects. She was most tenderly attached and even devoted to him, always preferring his gratification to her own. Her aged and beloved father, and a large circle of relatives and friends, she freely left to accompany her husband into England. For many years after she came to this country she still called New York her home, but she never requested or wished him to return'.

Elizabeth Frank gives a detailed account of Lindley's daily regimen, which varied little except for changes in health. He rose about seven o'clock, and when he was dressed he sat in an arm chair fitted with castors, in which Hannah pushed him to the sofa in the sitting-room, where he sat throughout the day. His meals were brought to him on a table. At other times a small stand with a writing desk on it was generally before him. The papers and books he was using were on the sofa at his side. Hannah sat on a chair beside him. The room was rather narrow, so the sofa was placed against the wall opposite the fire, to avoid draughts from doors and windows. The room had a window at each end, one looking south onto the garden; the other overlooked the turnpike road and fields with a path leading into the city. The fire was lit every day, even in summer, and the

*Lindley Murray's desk, now at The Mount School, York.*

windows were only opened before he came in. The temperature was kept around 65°F. After breakfast, Hannah or some other member of the household read from the bible or some other religious book. Before he became confined to the house he went out in his carriage from 12 to half-past one. Dinner at two was followed by a half-hour's siesta. Religious reading in the family, with meditation, closed the day. All the household went to bed at 10.

His diet was simple: breakfast and supper were of baked rice and milk or toast with milk, cocoa and bread; dinner consisted of meat, vegetables and pudding with a gill of porter (he never took spirits and seldom wine); in the afternoon he had half a cup of tea or fruit from the garden.

His time was spent largely in reading, writing and meditation. He kept up a regular and frequent correspondence with his relations in USA, and enjoyed reading a daily paper, taking a lively interest in public affairs. He also entertained visitors (including Maria Edgeworth and her father), and maintained an active interest in philanthropic work in York and beyond. He was often consulted on matters of law[3] and literature, morals and religion and the establishing and running of public institutions. He helped, for example, in making and maintaining a public footpath along the road from Holgate to York and had a seat placed by it. He helped the Bible Society, the African Institution and the schooling of poor children in Holgate; his will included bequests to the County Hospital, the Lunatic Asylum, the Dispensary, the Benevolent Society, the Blue Coat School for Boys and the Grey Coat School for Girls. The residue of his estate established a trust in the United States for charitable work for slaves and ex-slaves, Indians, the poor in general and for the distribution of religious books, particularly his own *Power of Religion on the Mind*.[4] He clearly retained a love of his native America to the end of his life; indeed John Griscom, who visited the Murrays in 1819 commented that though it was 34 years since they had left New York 'their feelings are still American'.

Lindley Murray's work with Friends, such as his membership of the Select Meeting of Ministers and Elders, his support for Esther Tuke's school in Trinity Lane[5] and for the founding of The Retreat,[6] and his encouragement to Friends to vote for William Wilberforce's election to Parliament,[7] is not mentioned by Elizabeth Frank, who seems to have been out of sympathy with his Quakerism. She writes:

> Mr. Murray was a member of the Society of Quakers or Friends, by whom he was much respected and esteemed and justly considered one of their brightest ornaments. From his earliest years he was educated in the principles of that Society to which he uniformly adhered. In his conduct and conversation, except in some instances in early life, he conformed to all the peculiarities of the sect, but always with his accustomed delicacy and regard to the feelings of others. Though attached to his own sect, he had a great respect for the truly religious persons of every denomination. He considered them and often spoke of them as members of one church, children of one holy and blessed family and fellow-travellers to a heavenly country. He regularly attended public worship as long as his health would permit, and often when his weakness and extreme susceptibility to cold rendered his attendance hazardous.

One of his American visitors commented that 'both he and Mrs. Murray have so tempered the strictness of the manners peculiar to their Society that they are polished people with the advantage of the utmost simplicity of deportment'.

To the end of his life, as health allowed, Lindley Murray was busy revising his Grammars 'to render them explicit and free from difficulty' and to meet criticisms which had been made; he also revised his other writings, including his Memoir, the revised version of which, made in 1823, Elizabeth Frank published on his death. He used to say that his books were his children and that he hoped they were well settled and doing good

THE
# POWER
OF
## RELIGION ON THE MIND,

IN

*RETIREMENT, AFFLICTION,*

AND

*AT THE APPROACH OF DEATH;*

Exemplified in the

TESTIMONIES AND EXPERIENCE

Of Persons distinguished by their

GREATNESS, LEARNING, OR VIRTUE.

---

'TIS IMMORTALITY,—'TIS THAT ALONE,
AMIDST LIFE'S PAINS, ABASEMENTS, EMPTINESS,
THE SOUL CAN COMFORT, ELEVATE, AND FILL........YOUNG.

---

By *LINDLEY MURRAY,*
Author of an English Grammar, &c. &c.

---

THE EIGHTEENTH EDITION, IMPROVED.

---

York:

Printed by Thomas Wilson and Sons, High-Ousegate;
FOR LONGMAN, HURST, REES, ORME, BROWN,
AND GREEN; FOR HARVEY AND DARTON, LONDON: AND
FOR WILSON AND SONS, YORK.

1825.

*(Price, bound, 5s.)*

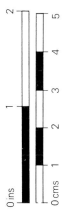

in the world – they occasioned him less trouble and anxiety than most children give their parents. He took a keen interest in the printing of his books, believing that good quality of paper and printing was important for their educational value. His sight and hearing remained good and he could read the smallest print with the aid of spectacles. His memory was remarkably retentive. He composed with speed and accuracy. His handwriting was uncommonly and uniformly neat. In fact he was neat and accurate in all he did.

Lindley Murray died in February 1826 at the age of 81, the last survivor of his siblings, and was buried in the Friends Burial Ground at Bishophill in York, where his better-known compatriot, John Woolman, had been buried 50 years earlier. Elizabeth Frank reports that there was a large gathering at the funeral, many having come from a considerable distance. She was struck by the Quaker burial service: 'From the stillness which prevailed one might have thought that only a few persons were present. All were silent and serious, many deeply affected'.

*Notes* *Chapter II*

[1] Lessons for Young Persons in Humble Life; A Friendly Gift for Servants and Apprentices; True Stories, or Anecdotes of Young Persons; True Stories, or Anecdotes of Children; Classical English Letter-writer; Arithmetic for Children. She joined Friends in 1798, but resigned in 1812. See L.M.'s remarks about her, Chap. III ad fin.

[2] A summer-house stood at the end of a gravel walk; he may well have worked on the Grammar in it. When the house was sold to the North Eastern Railway Co., the former owner, William Wilberforce Morrell presented it to The Mount School, where it still stands in the grounds. L.M.'s chair and writing desk are also in the possession of the School. See cover and pp. 38 and 41.

[3] He drafted a statement in defence of seven Friends from Lothersdale in Yorkshire, committed to York Castle in May 1795 and imprisoned for over two years for non-payment of tithes.

[4] His bequest of $30,500 established the Murray Fund, to be administered by trustees in New York. Its work still continues.

[5] He helped both with money and advice, and coached some of the young teachers in grammar; Hannah was one of the proprietors, who were all women Friends.

6 He joined with the Tukes in drawing up a prospectus for The Retreat in March 1792, and, according to Samuel Tuke, was 'amongst the most early and strenuous friends' of the hospital.
7 In 1806 William Tuke, Thomas Priestman and he produced a pamphlet, which recognised that Friends did not usually take an active part in elections, but stressed the importance of re-electing Wilberforce as a campaigner against the slave trade (see *The Tukes of York* by William K. & E. Margaret Sessions, p. 80).

> As a new Election of Members of Parliament for the County of York will soon commence, we take the liberty of recommending to the members of our society, who are entitled to vote on this occasion, to consider whether their late Representative William Wilberforce is not peculiarly entitled to their vote and interest. . . .
>
> We are sensible in general that it does not comport with the principles and practice of our society to take a very active part in elections, but there are occasions which call for such exertions . . . and we desire . . . to induce them to reflect on the great importance of re-electing a person whose labours have done so much towards abolishing the iniquitous trade in human beings . . . and whose continued exertions would greatly contribute to a happy termination of the wrongs and sorrows of Africa.
>
> WILLIAM TUKE
> THOMAS PRIESTMAN
> LINDLEY MURRAY
>
> YORK, 27th of 10th Month, 1806.

*Extracts from an Electioneering Pamphlet for William Wilberforce.*

CHAPTER III

# In His Correspondence

ELIZABETH FRANK faithfully carried out Lindley Murray's wishes that all his personal papers be destroyed; but his family kept some of his letters, mainly those to his brother John. These show a man devoted both to his own family and to Hannah's. Messages of affection came with every letter – to uncles and aunts, to nieces, nephews and cousins, and especially to his brother and sisters. Concern for health was unfailing, and occasional medical advice was offered: friction for rheumatism, or exercise and control of coughing for consumption. Sympathy for the bereaved was deeply felt and the consolation always offered of reunion in a better world. Continuing interest was shown in his brother John's children, in his namesake Lindley, and in the developing friendship of his niece Mary with Benjamin Perkins, which led to marriage and the birth of two children, soon to be fatherless through Benjamin's untimely death.

Affection was expressed in presents, such as a calico gown and a watch for sister Mary Willett or a carpet for his niece Mary Perkins. £30 a year was given to his sister Susan 'till her Beulah is older'. Two years' school fees were offered for his nephew Isaac Sharples, so that his father's death should not cut short his education.

Education was close to Lindley Murray's heart. He paid the school fees of Samuel Moore of Nova Scotia, following the report of his friend William Rotch, a travelling Quaker minister, and writes that he has 'been at considerable expense' for Judith Robertson,[1] sent to Ackworth in 1792, 'being of a disposition that would do much better abroad than at home'. The Murrays had hoped for 'much satisfaction from her society and assistance' (i.e. in their household), but she was now to be apprenticed to a dress-maker instead.

He took special interest in his nephew Lindley who wanted to become a bookseller; he was concerned that he continue his education at

*Holdgate, near York 30:th of 1:st mo: 1819.*

*My dear brother,*

*My Hannah and myself are concerned to have from thee so unfavourable an account of our dear niece, Mary Perkins. Remember us to her affectionately. I am desirous of recommending to her consideration, two prescriptions which it is not likely have been proposed to her. My advice is of a simple nature, and will, I believe, do no harm, if it does not prove useful. The first thing which I recommend is, to endeavour to suppress, or at least to soften, the coughing, as much as she can conveniently. The commencement of these exertions may be attended with considerable difficulty: but repeated trials will probably make them easier.*

The lungs may Thus, by degrees, become less irritated and torn. And this interval of composure may give them time to heal in some measure; and will likely diminish pain, promote sleep, increase appetite, and tend to tranquillize and invigorate other parts of the system, whose well being depends on a good state of the Lungs. – I believe that many persons have brought on consumptions, by hard coughing, and by yielding too much to the irritations of the lungs, which the cough is apt to occasion.

The second recommendation which I offer to my niece, is to use daily a certain exercise which may be called Hoisting, and is a motion of the arms similar to that which sailors use in pulling the ropes. I do not mean the use of a cord over a pulley, with a weight at the end of it: that might be too severe an exertion. But what I propose is, simply to raise the arms alternately over, or nearly over the head, as if a rope were pulled by the patient. The exercise might be varied by sometimes swinging the arms backwards and forwards, and sometimes by the motion similar to that of pulling a rope. This exercise expands the chest, gives motion to the lungs and other vital organs, and tends greatly to strengthen them. In particular, it disposes the lungs to throw off and disperse the offending matter which oppresses and adheres to them, and which prevents their free and natural operations. If our dear Mary should be inclined to try this exercise, she might begin with it for a minute or two minutes at a time, three or four times a day; and gradually increase it, as she may be able, till she can continue the exercise for eight or ten minutes at one time, twice a day, or oftener, if she finds it to agree with her. It would be proper to sit down, after each time of exercise, both to rest, and to encourage the glow or warmth if any should be produced. She should persevere in this exertion, and in her endeavours to suppress, in some degree, her cough, unless she perceives clearly that, after a fair trial, they do not suit her case. Perhaps one may agree with her, if both do not. – This practice of hoisting, and of swinging the arms, is, I think, well adapted to cure or relieve disorders of the Liver, as well as to be of use in consumptive cases.

*Letter to John Murray of New York regarding Mary Perkin's ailment.*

Burlington Monthly Meeting School in a wide range of subjects, especially French, Latin and Greek, which he commended several times: if he had no occasion to use them in the future they would 'make him better acquainted with his native tongue and promote habits of attention, quickness and discrimination'.

He supported Ackworth from his arrival in York and regarded it as the model for other Friends Schools, describing Westtown (founded in 1799, 20 years after Ackworth) as 'the Ackworth near Philadelphia'. When in 1796 New York Yearly Meeting established a boarding school about 80 miles north of New York in the Nine Partners Monthly Meeting area (now Oakwood School) he showed keen interest in the planning, and stressed the importance of starting on the right lines: 'In this work you may very naturally look to Ackworth as a perfect model'. He sent financial help, and rejoiced that the school prospered. He was amazed that some Friends should object to Quaker education: 'The idea that ignorance is the mother of devotion or the source of subordination can at this day exist only in very short-sighted persons'. Many Friends were still hostile to religious teaching, believing that all should come directly from the spirit.

He was keen to be kept in touch with Friends in New York and Philadelphia, both individually and in their collective concerns. He asked for a copy of the New York Book of Discipline, and was upset when this was refused. He was particularly troubled at the views of Hannah Barnard, a travelling American minister, who questioned some aspects of the Old Testament, e.g. the passages approving of war, and he supported her chief opponent, another travelling American minister, David Sands. He followed lovingly the travels of Quaker ministers from England, such as his friends Martha Routh, William Crotch and Ann Alexander, and gave his brother news of York Friends and of the visits of American Friends to York. He asked John to help a young Friend from Hull, a sailor, when he came to New York, and urged that Friends care for a party of seven Seneca Indians, who had visited him in York, on their return to the States.

He was eager for news on public affairs, and asked John for information on state prisons, on hospitals and on negro affairs, and on individuals active in public life. He reported on the decision of the House of Commons to abolish the Slave Trade (1792), giving details of the voting. He was interested in pamphlets against war and in the effect of Christian appeals on the subject to the people of America. When, in 1807, a British warship seized an American frigate, he was apprehensive that this might cause a rupture between America and Britain – John was to remember that he was registered in Britain as an American citizen under the Aliens Act, so that his property in New York should not be liable to seizure. He later expressed fear of war following the return to France in 1813 of 'that disturber of nations, the insatiably ambitious and faithless Napoleon'.

His brother John managed his financial affairs in America, where most of his capital was invested. He was usually very grateful for this service, but occasionally administered quite tart reprimands, e.g. for not sending him regular accounts, or for being in a hurry to enlarge his business. Disapproval sometimes was expressed in warnings about the 'subtle adversary' we face: 'Ah my dear brother! There is nothing can preserve us from the artifices of the Grand Destroyer but obedience to that still small voice, which speaks to persuade, not to compel us. The more we listen, the more we hear; and the greater our obedience, the stronger we grow'. John had to deal with their uncle over the settling of their father's estate, an embarrassing business; Lindley was upset over their uncle's unpaid debts, and remarked, 'I wonder how you can be easy with it'. He disapproved, too, of some of John's actions, such as offering to sell the family home to a sitting tenant.

The delay and uncertainty of the mail – letters normally took about two months and often were lost – made it difficult for him to retain the oversight he wished. He felt frustrated, and complained, 'I have no more than sufficient for my present support . . . and my infirmities have put it entirely out of my power to do any sort of business'. This appeal to his ill-health was unfair; he always seemed to have been comfortably off. His publications could have been a good source of income, but he preferred to give away the money he made to charity. He sold his copyrights to his English publishers on terms which greatly favoured them, and made no money out of his American editions, being more concerned that his books should be used than that they should be profitable.

He was nevertheless a careful business man, e.g. objecting to the sale of any of his houses when real estate was 'advancing' (1793). He was careful of small sums too, e.g. questioning whether the £20 for widow Taylor should not have made more than $95.88 at the current exchange rate. He protested over excessive postal charges and wrote to London about it, getting 33/1d reduced to 10/6d and £3/8/9 to a guinea. He urged that parcels be made up to the limit of 12 lbs. as that cost 'no more than 12 oz.'

John may not have appreciated all the advice he received, as when Lindley used all his legal knowledge to explain the pitfalls that partnerships involved – John went ahead all the same. For similar reasons he was not to 'invest with any relation, as that may be attended with difficulties'. He must keep exact accounts, and make a satisfactory will: 'It is of consequence to provide wisely and timely'. All houses should be '*fully insured*'. He was to be surety to no one whatever for a greater amount than he could bear to lose, nor to lend his name or engage with another so that it could be construed in law as a partnership. 'Be exceedingly careful,' Lindley advised, 'that thou dost not spend a shilling more in the year than the amount of thy clear income, after deducting all losses and charges'. Hannah was told, similarly, never to break into capital, but only to give help with what could be spared from annual income, so that she would not encroach upon the principal either in England or New York.

Lindley encouraged the publication and circulation of his books with great energy. He sent parcels to be distributed as presents to friends and people of importance. Instructions were repeatedly sent on the proper packing of books in boxes, on notifying details of posting and on collecting parcels from ships when they docked. Damage or loss was not infrequent; sometimes parcels were entrusted to private passengers as a safer method of transport.

Arrangements were made for bookseller-publishers to reprint his works in America, and care was taken that they should use the most recent editions with all the latest corrections and improvements. Firms in New York and Philadelphia were used, but sometimes he gave his books to publishers in other towns as well. Benjamin Johnson and Collins & Perkins, both of Philadelphia, produced his works regularly. On one occasion Collins was given one month's preference to reprint the second edition of the Sequel, but usually all firms had equal rights to publish. Some pirating took place; Lindley did not react strongly, though he observed that he disliked this method of obtaining copyright. He sent his books for review to magazines like *The American Gazette*, and urged his publishers to print good notices ('characters') in his books, as his English publishers had found that this stimulated sales. He asked to see copies of the American editions and to be told how they were selling. He was pleased at the report that his books were 'extensively used in the best schools' and asked which of them were in use at Westtown, commenting that *The Compendium* was being used at Ackworth.

Some reviews were critical and he was attacked by Noah Webster for plagiarism, a criticism he strenuously denied; but he would not allow others to reply on his behalf.

He of course gave regular accounts of his (and Hannah's) state of health. Soon after reaching England in 1785 he reported to his father that he could 'sit meetings', and drive 20 miles a day, but could not walk more than 10 or 12 times across the room without feeling weak for several

A

# COMPENDIUM

OF

*Religious Faith and Practice.*

DESIGNED

## FOR YOUNG PERSONS

OF

## THE SOCIETY OF FRIENDS.

By *LINDLEY MURRAY.*

𝕳𝖔𝖗𝖐 :

Printed for W. ALEXANDER, and sold by him :
sold also by
M. M. and E. WEBB, Bristol; DARTON, HARVEY, and CO.;
W. PHILLIPS, and W. DARTON, Jun. London.

1815.

hours. He was at times very weak, and as Elizabeth Frank says was subject to colds, but in 1795 was still driving out each day and attending meetings. But 10 years later he rarely went out, his voice was feeble and he complained of rheumatism in the small of the back and had difficulty getting out of bed and dressing. In 1808 the daily drives were resumed 'in a close carriage', but next year he was confined to the house as driving 'in a hardgoing carriage increased his debility'. He was therefore confined to sittingroom and bedroom unable to walk more than a few steps. In 1818 he made the experiment of going out in a sedan chair, but found the confined space too hot.

Hannah suffered from headaches and colic; she was at first able to walk into York and back, a distance of about two miles, but by 1813 she too was confined to the house.

Lindley responded to John's request in 1801 for a description of the menage at Holgate House. His account may be compared with Elizabeth Frank's:

> My family is but small: 3 in the parlour and 3 in the kitchen. In the parlour, my wife, Elizabeth Frank and myself: in the kitchen, a man servant, a housemaid and a chamber maid, the latter assists my wife in sewing, her eyes not allowing her to do much in that line. I keep a close carriage and pair of horses from necessity; and the above-mentioned man servant drives and is my gardener. I have a neat 3 storied house, and a pleasant garden. My sitting room is pretty large, with a bow window at each end, one looking into the garden, and the other towards a fine verdant hill about two hundred yards distant. Our house is dry, and the village we live in remarkably healthy, as it consists of a gravelly soil. My state of health does not admit of our having but very little *dining* company. We, however, have many friends who *take tea*, and spend the afternoons with us. Few friends from other parts of the country come to York without calling to see us; by which means, in the course of sixteen years, we have formed an acquaintance with some friends in most parts of the nation. We keep a frugal table. No delicacies, but plenty of good wholesome food. Our garden furnishes our vegetables; and a field of 3 acres, within 50 yards of our house, grazing for the horses. This is our mode of living.
>
> The young woman that resides with us is named Elizabeth Frank. She has been in our family about seven years, and is about 28 years of age. She is of a respectable family, her father a justice of the Peace, and a man of large property. She is a well bred woman, well educated, and

HOLDGATE, NEAR YORK,
*The Residence of the late Mr Lindley Murray*

*Holdgate House still stands on Holgate Road, (now spelt without the d). This crosses one end of Dalton Terrace, where The Mount School moved from Castlegate in 1857.*

very sensible. Our acquaintance commenced from her living in lodgings at a neighbouring village for a time. She often visited us; and on finding her not satisfied with her situation, we invited her to take up her residence with us. She has two rooms to herself; and as she would not consent to board with us, without some suitable acknowledgement, we receive from her a yearly sum, as nearly as we can judge equal to what we furnish, without any gain.

*Note*  *Chapter III*

[1] John was interested in her as she came from New York. She was born 10.3.78, and entered Ackworth on William Tuke's recommendation; she left on 27.2.89 with Elizabeth Taylor, perhaps as her apprentice.

*Holdgate House from the garden, 1827.*

CHAPTER IV
# Lindley the Friend

LINDLEY MURRARY was brought up in a Quaker home, the child of Quaker parents; his father read the Bible daily to the family, as was the Quaker custom; the children attended Meeting for Worship and learned to value the teaching and example of leading Quakers. But in all his writings he studiously avoids the terms 'Quaker' and 'Friend'. This may be partly explained by the sense of privacy many Friends felt about the affairs of the Society, and by the fact that most of his writings were intended for the general public on topics of general interest. His first publication, *The Power of Religion on the Mind*, was anonymous, and was strictly non-denominational, as he was concerned to appeal to Christians generally. His choice of examples to illustrate his theme of the need for religious faith in facing death only includes one Quaker, Anthony Benezet, and he does not mention that he was a Friend. He picks Admiral Penn, rather than his son William, whose words on death are still valued by many Friends and are quoted in the *Christian Faith and Practice of London Y.M.* (1959).

This absence of specific Quakerism from his writings may also be partly due to his natural reticence. As Elizabeth Frank has said he left instructions for all his personal papers to be destroyed and only agreed to write his reminiscences with some reluctance, under pressure from a close friend. He apologises for the necessity this involved of using 'the objectionable pronoun' "I". It was too a feature of the times to write allusively rather than directly. Thus he talks of attending divine worship, when we would say going to Meeting. Similarly he prefers to speak of the deity as Divine Providence rather than as God.[1]

Yet it is hard to resist the conclusion that he was not keen to advocate the distinctive practices and testimonies of Quakerism. He would not understand the modern tendency to value the silence for itself; for him it was the public worship of God that was important – the fact that he worshipped in silence and that women could minister as well as men were not points he wished to emphasise, as if they were parts of his personal way of life on which the outside world should not intrude. The character of his outlook can be judged from his Introduction to his *Compendium of Religious Faith and Practice, designed for young persons of the Society of Friends* (1815), the only work he wrote which was specifically intended for Friends. After reminding his young readers of their good fortune in being brought up in a country where Christianity prevailed and the Scriptures were known in their original purity, he goes on, 'Besides this privilege, in common with young persons of other religious denominations, you have had the peculiar advantage of being educated in a Society of Christians, whose principles teach them great moderation in all their desires and pursuits, whose manners and habits of life preserve them from many evils; and who so highly recommend love towards their fellow-beings, as to disapprove of all wars and fightings, contentions and animosities; and who are particularly careful to guard their members, especially their youth, against those customs, fashions, and diversions of the world, which are apt to insnare [sic] and corrupt the mind, dispose it by insensible degrees, to slight, if not to reject, the pure, self-denying doctrines of the Gospel'. He also prefaced the work with a note explaining that he had not felt it appropriate to include 'all the peculiar doctrines of the Society' or to explain 'with much particularity' those which he had included – and this in a book addressed specifically to young Friends.

These passages illustrate a view of Quakerism which was typical of the period.[2] It would follow, for example, that the 'guarded education' which was to be provided in the Friends' Schools being established at this time (and several were founded by Lindley Murray's generation and that which followed it) was not intended to protect the Quakerism of Friends' children. The young of the Society were not to be 'guarded' against corruption by the tenets and practices of other denominations, but against the irreligious world. It was not Quakerism that was to be advanced, particularly, but Christianity. The modern idea that Friends' Schools should be used for Quaker outreach would have seemed narrow and parochial. Lindley Murray, of course, contributed both advice and money to the Friends' school being run by his friends the Tukes in Trinity Lane, but he was no less concerned for the education of children in his village of Holgate and in York generally.

Many Friends no longer thought of themselves as 'a peculiar people'. The Murrays clearly played down their Quaker peculiarities where they might embarrass visitors. They welcomed those causes like the anti-slavery movement and the work of the Bible Society in which they

# 1784
## PROPOSED
# BOARDING - SCHOOL FOR GIRLS
## At YORK.

THE EDUCATION of FRIENDS CHILDREN in general, eſpecially Girls, conſiſtent with the Principles we profeſs, having been the ſubject of ſolid conſideration with divers Friends, who have beheld with ſatisfaction the advantages derived from A C K W O R T H   S C H O O L , and are deſirous that a ſimilar opportunity of a guarded Education may be extended to ſuch Girls, who, by reaſon of their Age, or on account of the circumſtances of their Parents or Friends, are not ſent thither.

In order to promote an eſtabliſhment ſo beneficial to the Society, the following Friends propose to open a S C H O O L at Y O R K , viz.

| ESTHER TUKE | § | TABITHA MIDDLETON |
| MARTHA ROUTH | § | SARAH GRUBB |
| MARY PROUD | § | SARAH SWANWICK |
| ANN NORTH | § | ELIZABETH HOYLAND |
| SARAH PRIESTMAN | § | |

with a hope that, if the Inſtitution is found to anſwer the deſired end, other Friends will, after the deceaſe of any of them, unite with the Survivors for its continuance and ſupport.

The School is intended to be opened the 1ſt of 1ſt month., 1785, under the immediate inſpection of Eſther Tuke, and occaſionally of others of the aforeſaid Friends. Suitable Teachers to be provided for inſtructing the Children in uſeful Needlework, Knitting, the Engliſh Language, Writing, and Arithmetic.

The terms for Board, Waſhing, and Education, will be 14 Guineas a year, to be paid at Entrance; Waſhing of Gowns and Frocks not included.

None to be taken for leſs than one year; but if any thing extraordinary ſhould render their removal neceſſary before the expiration of that time, money to be returned for the remaining full quarters.

In order that plainneſs and moderation, conſiſtent with our religious Principles, may be attended to in the Education of theſe Children, it is requeſted that ſuch apparel as is coſtly, or ſuperfluous, may be avoided: alſo ſuch kinds as cauſe extraordinary trouble in waſhing.

*The forerunner of The Mount School in Trinity Lane, York 1784. Hannah Murray became one of the proprietors shortly after the school opened.*

worked with other Christians. They had not yet reached the position of evangelicals like Joseph John Gurney, but they were moving towards it.

This is illustrated by the comparative rareness of Lindley's references to Christ. He mentions in his Memoirs 'those who truly repent and believe in Jesus Christ the Redeemer of the World', through whose atonement and intercession God would 'pardon all their sins and prepare them by the operation of his Holy Spirit for an admittance to his blessed kingdom' (p. 116). This thought, with its trinitarian formulation, is repeated in the statement of faith with which he concludes the Memoir, though he there has an original reference to belief in 'Christ, pardon and peace'. His sister Mary, whose last days he describes in some detail, seems to have come closer to evangelical formulations than he did, according to his own account. She responded, for example, to someone who remarked that they wanted to 'take pattern after her': 'I desire to take pattern after the Lord Jesus Christ.' She told her husband: 'I believe I have been favoured with the sweet spirit of my blessed Saviour', and her last words were, 'Sweet Jesus, take me to thyself'. Lindley is clearly moved by his sister's testimony, but he never expresses his faith in so Christ-centred a way.

This is further illustrated by the emphasis in his *Compendium of Religious Faith and Practice*, which begins its first chapter (Articles of Faith, or What we are to believe) with 10 paragraphs on the nature of God and his plan for humanity. God is described, at some length, as the Maker and Preserver of all things, as eternal and unchangeable, all-powerful and glorious, omnipresent and omniscient; a God of truth, holiness and justice, of wisdom, love and mercy, possessing all perfection. Though he is one, yet there exists in him 'the mysterious union of the Father, the Son, and the Holy Spirit'. He created us that 'we might glorify, love and serve Him for ever and find our happiness in these duties'. All are involved in the consequences of Adam's transgression; he sent 'his dear and only Son, the expected Messiah, to atone for our sins and reconcile the world to Himself'.

This is followed by four paragraphs on 'Redemption by Jesus Christ' in which 'The Lord Jesus Christ' is described as 'this compassionate Redeemer' and 'the great Head of the universal Church'; the title 'Lord and Master' is used of God. He then expounds the plan of salvation: we cannot save ourselves from sin and misery; only by the grace of God in Jesus Christ can we obey him and be made fit for happiness in our future life, for after death there will be 'a state of rewards and punishments, a great day of final judgment'. 'Those who have true faith, who sincerely repent of their sins and serve God acceptably will be happy for ever.' Reference to 'true faith in God and in the Lord Jesus Christ' is made in several later sections. It is noteworthy that he regards the Holy Spirit as 'purchased by Jesus Christ for all mankind'; it is only by his gift that we are enlightened and directed – he never speaks of 'that of God in every man'.

Quaker emphases appear in the Section on the Ministry of the Gospel which requires the influence of the Holy Spirit and is open to women as well as men, and in the section on Baptism and the Lord's Supper which 'appear to be wholly of a spiritual nature, unmixed with any ceremonial or outward observances. But to those who view these subjects differently, our Christian charity is especially due'.

Similarly, the Articles on Practice begin with duties towards God, 'awe and veneration . . . a solemn sense of his continual presence and a fear to offend Him', love and trust, gratitude and obedience, frequent waiting upon God and fervent prayer for the pardon of sins and for grace. True worship is 'inward and spiritual' and is required both in private and in public. Regular attendance at Meetings for Worship is stressed, both for silent prayer, thanksgiving and praise, and for the vocal ministry of those led by the Holy Spirit in 'exhortation, prayer, thanksgiving or praise'. Patience and resignation to the will of God and trust in His goodness are enjoined, as are being affectionate and dutiful to parents, obeying the laws of one's country 'when they do not oppose the law of God', sincere love for others – and hence avoiding all wars and fightings, forgiving those who wrong us, being just and honest in all our dealings, respecting truth and avoiding 'tale-bearing and detraction', refusing to swear on oath, relieving the needs of the poor.

An ecumenical spirit is encouraged: 'Though we ought to value the privileges peculiar to us, and firmly maintain the religious tenets which we most approve, we ought to cherish sentiments of charity and Christian regard, towards those who conscientiously differ from us'. Much of the Quaker way of life was, in fact, shared by many other Christians, as in abstaining from intemperance in 'the use of meats and drinks', avoiding 'all prohibited and improper indulgence of the senses, all vain customs and fashions, diversions and pleasures of the world'; but Quakers may still have had a particular care to avoid extravagance 'in our furniture and way of living, our dress and language and in all amusements and deportment' and to shun 'every species of flattery'. Other Christians were no doubt also encouraged to seek the friendship of the virtuous and pious and avoid those who are 'vicious and irregular in their conduct', and to read good and useful books, especially the Bible, for 'the reading of light and frivolous publications tends to enfeeble and corrupt the mind'.

Every Section of The Compendium is illustrated by numerous Bible quotations, for the teachings of Holy Scripture, 'communicated by a

Being of infinite wisdom, are to be devoutly believed by us', though 'our frail reason' may not be able to comprehend and explain them all. Young Friends were expected to learn all Murray's text by heart, as well as the Scripture quotations, and he appends a form of catechism so that they could be tested (using the same method as for learning grammar). Friends had been hostile to specific religious teaching, even to the study of the Bible. But attitudes were changing: Samuel Tuke records a visit he paid to Lindley Murray (16.10.1814) during which they discussed 'the religious instruction of youth' and the objection of 'some persons' to the use of external means. Lindley maintained that 'it was our duty to use all reasonable means to obtain the end proposed, and then to pray and hope for a blessing on those means', and he quotes Paul's injunction to Timothy to 'stir up the gift in him' (II *Tim.* 1.6). He thought it right 'to prejudice or bias children's minds on these subjects, not to leave their future adoption or rejection to chance; nor did he think it any reason against their inculcation that children would not fully comprehend them'.

He thus adopted the same authoritarian philosophy in religion as he did in the writing and speaking of English. Correct beliefs and correct idiom were both to be taught by an intensive process of memorisation. We cannot judge the success of his method. The Society of Friends in Britain sank to its lowest ebb numerically in the two generations following the publication of the Compendium in 1815. But then he was not trying to make children into Quakers; nor do we know how far his method was applied. His authoritarianism was not, in fact, as mechanical as his principal method suggests. He knew from his own experience as a youth that teenagers were not to be coerced; he therefore stressed that one must 'consult the inclinations, genius and bodily constitutions of young people seeking employment'. His concern too that children should be taught 'veneration' for Scripture, and pleasure in reading it, was to be achieved by example, not by rote, and by seizing 'occasions of presenting Holy Scripture to them under favourable and inviting points of view'.

Modern Friends will feel more in tune with his friendly attitude towards other denominations and with his active involvement in social work, on which he spent the money he earned from the success of his writings. Like John Woolman, he withdrew from business when he had accumulated enough capital on which to live in reasonable comfort. This was, he said, 'to devote a great part of my time, in some way or other, to the benefit of my fellow-creatures'.

But we would not have felt comfortable in his Meetings for Worship, any more than he would in ours. He would miss the confidence of ministering Friends, proclaiming the gospel from the Ministers' Gallery and would regard our insistence on the primacy of personal experience as a shaky foundation for religious faith. We might comment that it is not so easy to exclude personal experience from the formulation of our faith; the Scripture passages Lindley Murray selected as examples for young Friends to learn were those which appealed to him as expressing what he believed. He might, in reply, ask us if we have not gone too far in reducing the influence the Bible has on the life and thought of our Society.

But his contribution as a Friend cannot be judged only from his books. He was a valued member of the Meeting – he and Hannah were appointed elders in 1787. It had been an important criterion for him in choosing where to settle to find a place where they could 'derive comfort and some degree of religious strength from the society and example of good and pious persons', which was his way of saying, near a good Meeting. York fully met his hopes; he counted membership of the Meeting 'as one of the greatest blessings of our lives'.

The Tukes had been quick to make the Murrays welcome. William helped with the purchase of the house, and indeed may have sought Lindley out to help them with their educational plans. He must have spoken acceptably in Meeting, for he was recorded a minister in 1791; when he became too feeble physically for vocal ministry, he returned to being an elder (1802). He was thus able to continue as a member of the Select Meeting (of ministers and elders), where Esther Tuke had valued his presence so much that she declared that, if he became unable through ill-health to get to the meetings, the meeting must go to him.

He made the largest contribution of any Friend in the Meeting to the Meeting collections, which were at agreed rates based on ability to pay: in the list revised in 1795 Lindley paid the top rate of 7/6 and John Fothergill the lowest at 2/-. He subscribed regularly to Ackworth, and contributed to the new Meeting House at Leeds. He served on the committee to revise the list of collections, and was appointed representative to Monthly Meeting and to the Quarterly Meeting of Ministers and Elders as his health permitted.[3] He was respected as a man of education and experience and his advice was often sought; as a good friend, he was much loved, and gladly visited, as his illness more and more confined him to his room.

One such visit is described by Maria Tuke, daughter of Samuel Tuke, writing to her children:

> Our dear papa loved L.M. very much and like[s] to take us to see him. Sometimes when dinner was over he would say, 'We are going to take tea at Holgate [the place where Lindley Murray lived] and we can take two or three of you with us'. When we got to Holgate we

were taken into a small sitting room, and a lady named Hannah Richardson[4] came to us with a pleasant smiling face, and told us how pleased she was to see us; and when we were all ready, she took us into the room where Lindley Murray was. Our mamma went in first, and we followed one by one, and went up to the chair where he was sitting, and shook hands with him. He did not get up for he could not walk. His wife sat by him in a little black bonnet; a sweet gentle-looking little woman she was. Our papa sat on the other side of L.M.; and then our mamma was placed beside his wife on a hard sofa covered with green stuff; and we were placed on chairs in a line with it, for it was a very long room. We sat very still, looking first out of the window at one end of the room into the old-fashioned garden, and then out of the other window which looked into the pleasant road and over the green fields. Sometimes Hannah Richardson talked to us; and she went to a little dark mahogany corner cupboard and brought out a little plate of Savoy biscuits which she handed to us.

In a little while the door opened and Mary came in with the tea. The tea-pot was not made of silver, for Lindley Murray would not have anything but spoons of silver; he thought Christian people ought not to use costly things and spend a great deal of money to make themselves grand or even very comfortable; he thought they ought to spend it on those who are poor and need help. Well, the cups and saucers were soon on the table, cups without handles, as they were made in former times; and then Mary brought in the tray of very nice hot tea-cakes, and set the chairs, and when she saw us all seated, she went and sat down herself with a waiter in her hand on a chair behind us, to be ready if anything was wanted.

After tea Hannah Richardson said in a cheerful voice, 'Now I daresay the children will like to go into the garden'. We were very glad when she said this; so we got up directly and walked out of the room, looking very grave; but as soon as we were left alone on the broad straight gravel walk which went quite to the other end of the long garden, we began to run and laugh. We went to the nice summer-house[5] which had a door and many windows in it, and a table and chairs, all painted white, and as clean as could be. When Henry [elder brother of Maria] was with us he drew queer things on this clean white table, for he was so fond of drawing that if he had a pencil he could hardly help using it.

Sometimes we peeped into the kitchen where Mary[6] was making tea for Robert who drove us here, and who had put up the horse and

*Lindley Murray's Summerhouse presented to The Mount School, York in 1901 by William Wilberforce Morrell. (Note the original finial.)*

carriage in the old coach-house and stable. Mary was very kind. She was dressed like a very plain Friend, and when we went into the kitchen she would say, 'Well, sure my dears, I am very glad to see you.'

When we had amused ourselves awhile in the garden, Hannah Richardson came to fetch us to read to Lindley Murray. Now we were very much afraid of this, but we could not disobey; so we walked again into the room, one by one, and our papa took a book from the round bookshelves near the window, and called us in our turns to stand by him and read. Lindley Murray had a grave face but a kind one; and he stroked our heads when we had done and thanked us for reading to him. But our papa used to say, 'No, they should be obliged to thee for hearing them read.' Then we had the Savoy biscuits handed again, and put on our things, and Robert brought the carriage to the gate.

Lindley Murray may well strike us now as an uncongenial figure, whether we view him through the pages of his Grammar or of his Compendium. We can no longer approach either the study of English or the expression of our faith in his way. Yet we must admit that his way had considerable appeal in his time. His life bears testimony to the validity of his faith; for he bore without complaint the restrictions of a debilitating illness, which robbed him of the physical activity he so much enjoyed and, in later years, of all contact with others, except for correspondents and visitors. Only once, he tells us, did he repine at his situation, and that was in the first year of the illness, when the medicine prescribed did him harm instead of providing relief. He accepted his trials as a spiritual discipline, and such, no doubt, it proved. He certainly would wish an account of his life to end with thanks to Divine Providence, from which all good things come, and in his case particularly the unfailing loving care of Hannah.

*Notes* *Chapter IV*

[1] The Advices to Ministers and Elders, first published in 1783, warned against 'too often repeating the high and holy name' of God.
[2] A close parallel is provided by Henry Tuke's *Principles of Religion* (1805), which became the standard interpretation of Quakerism; it went through 12 English editions by the middle of the century and was frequently reissued in

the different American Yearly Meetings. 'There was hardly a single Quaker home which did not own a copy' (Rufus Jones, *Later Periods of Quakerism*, p. 287).

[3] Hannah was a regular attender at business meetings; she was often a representative to Monthly Meeting between 1786 and 1809, and served as elder and later as overseer. She visited on applications for membership, and was appointed to deal with a woman Friend thought to be intending to make an unsuitable marriage. She served on committees, e.g. 'to inspect the case of Friends in low circumstances' and to nominate overseers, elders and ministers.

[4] She had succeeded Elizabeth Frank in 1814 and lived with the Murrays as housekeeper-companion till Hannah's death in 1834. Born in 1783, she was a daughter of Henry and Hannah (Priestman) Richardson of Stockton on Tees. Mrs. Boyce in her *Richardsons of Cleveland* records how every morning her tall, lissom figure was seen on the road between Holdgate and York, her feet shod with pattens if the weather was wet, her hand carrying a basket, her walk full of energy and directness of purpose. It is still remembered how her coming was watched for in houses which she passed in her daily walk; and how her friends would rush to door or window to beg for a few minutes of her company; but, beyond the time required for loving greetings and inquiries, she might not prolong her stay. The invalid almost counted the minutes until her return with his letters, his daily paper, his *Newcastle Chronicle* once a week, and the news of his friends. She went to Ackworth in 1836 and served for 10 years as 'Governess', i.e. in charge of the girls.

[5] See Chap. II, note 2.
[6] Mary Hollingworth.

THE

**Principles of Religion,**

AS PROFESSED BY THE

SOCIETY OF CHRISTIANS,

USUALLY CALLED

Q U A K E R S.

Written for the Instruction of their YOUTH, and for the Information of STRANGERS.

By HENRY TUKE.

THE THIRD EDITION.

LONDON:
PRINTED AND SOLD BY
*PHILLIPS* AND *FARDON*,
GEORGE YARD,
LOMBARD STREET.

1805.

Price 2s. 6d. in BOARDS.

CHAPTER V

# Murray the Grammarian

THE PHENOMENAL SUCCESS OF *The English Grammar* has given Lindley Murray a place in the history of English education and in the development of text-book publication. Yet he made no claim to originality; his work is based on previous grammars, as he freely admits in his Introduction, naming the writers to whom he was principally indebted (Harris, Johnson, Lowth, Priestley, Beattie, Sheridan, Walker and Coote). He regularly refers to himself as 'the compiler'. His aim is to adapt the work of his predecessors to the needs of schoolchildren, and to do so in a way that might inculcate 'piety and virtue'.

His quotation from Blair on the title-page shows that he regarded the study of grammar as more than a matter of learning correct usage: the ability to think 'with accuracy and order' would develop from learning to speak and write accurately. He quotes also Quintilian's comment that 'they who penetrate into the innermost parts of this temple of science will there discover such refinement and subtlety of matter as are not only proper to sharpen the understandings of young persons, but sufficient to give exercise for the most profound knowledge and erudition'.

Murray constantly has in mind the use of his book by students of different ages and capacities – the original work was designed both for teachers and their pupils; hence the distinction made by printing the basic material in larger type and subsidiary rules and discussions in smaller. The former was published separately as *The Abridgement* and this was the form in which the Grammar was chiefly studied in schools, as is shown by the fact that it ran to 131 editions between 1797 and 1859, compared with 58 of the standard duodecimo edition (1795-1867) and eight of the splendid octavo, intended as a reference book for adults.

In detail also he keeps his readers in mind: for example, he omits derivations from Greek and Latin, as many may not know these languages; he rejects new theories, e.g. on tenses, though these might be improvements grammatically, because they might be confusing to those familiar with the established system. The book was intended to be used as a handbook for exercises in parsing (which he himself had enjoyed as a schoolboy in Philadelphia); hence he excludes the common gender, as it is unnecessary for parsing, but admits the objective case, with some reluctance, as teachers find it helpful – he emphasises that it is for the purpose of parsing only.

He inclines naturally to principles of moderation, as he admits: 'those who endeavour to improve our language should observe a happy medium between too great and too little reverence for usages of ancient time'. He disliked innovation which would 'deviate from the established terms and arrangements,' partly at least because it was confusing for teachers and their pupils. He resisted new terminology, even though 'the old terms might not be exactly significant of their nature and distinctions', e.g. preferring the conventional six tenses to Harris's 12: it was more useful 'to take the tenses as they are commonly received and endeavour to ascertain their nature and their differences'. He did, however, generally adopt 'noun' for 'substantive'.

He believed that 'the practice of the best writers, corroborated by general usage' was the proper criterion of correctness. Hence anomalies and variations could well be correct: 'it is the grammarian's duty to submit (sc. to common usage), not to remonstrate' on grounds of analogy, derivation or propriety. Thus he allows *from* with the words *hence, whence, thence,* which might seem grammatically wrong; but to omit *from* 'would seem stiff'. Words and constructions must be 'national, reputable and present', 'national' meaning neither provincial nor foreign, and 'reputable' having the esteem of the public in their acceptance of the authors of the day. But he distinguishes between what is allowable 'in common conversation', e.g. ending a sentence with a preposition, and what belongs to 'the solemn and elevated style'.

He also goes by what sounds better, e.g. on the position of adverbs, 'it is the easy flow and perspicuity of the phrases which ought to be chiefly regarded'. An adjective may follow a noun if it 'gives a better sound'. But sound is a secondary consideration, even in style where it is important 'to attend to the harmony and easy flow of the words and members': 'in no instance should perspicuity, precision or strength be sacrificed to sound'. Despite his definition of grammar as the art of speaking as well as of writing, his thought, especially in his advice on style, is of formal writing.

Murray tried to formulate rules in accordance with 'the genius of the English language'. He accepted the idea of a universal grammar, by which, for example, a system of moods applied to all languages, though it was expressed in different ways in different languages. Hence declining a noun as in Latin and Greek grammar does not 'suit the idiom of our language'. He protests against applying the principles of Latin and Greek grammars to English.

English grammars had originally been designed to conform to Latin rules, e.g. by Lily and Colet (1509), and the main interest for many was to help pupils in learning their Latin. Locke called for English to be studied in schools before Latin, but English grammar was slow to gain acceptance as a school subject. The first English grammars for schools did not appear till 1734 (Loughton's Practical Grammar of the English Tongue). The spirit of the 18th century favoured emphasis on logic and rules, and this prescriptive attitude marked Lowth's Short Introduction to English Grammar (1762), which became the model till it was replaced by Murray. Priestley, approaching the subject from a scientific background, maintained that usage should be the main criterion (1761, 1762), but met with little support.

Murray was also moving towards a functional theory – that the parsing of a word depends, not on its general categorisation, but on its function in its particular context. Thus a word like 'much' may be used as an adjective or an adverb or a noun – only its sense in the particular context can determine its parsing. But he kept the terminology of logical and formalistic writers, e.g. 'case', which he admits refers to the terminations of words and therefore has limited application in English. He adopts the objective case because it shows the function of nouns after active verbs.

If the *English Grammar* is essentially a compilation, it is also a discriminating selection of the material available. Murray uses the form of rigid rules and classification because that was the only system practised, but his view is not as prescriptive as his forerunners'; he sees the grammarian, not as lawgiver, but as observer of common usage. He did not think it necessary for children to understand, because he believed them not yet capable of rational reflection. John Dalton criticised the Grammar as 'a perplexing book for children's brains'. Rules were to be memorised and applied in exercises. Understanding would come gradually, for the process developed capacity for thought, the primary object of the study of grammar. He emphasised also that rules were not rigid or absolute and often needed to be qualified by exceptions. In the case of punctuation, for example, he admitted that few rules could be given which were free from exceptions: 'much must be left to the judgment and taste of the reader'.

It is hard to judge how far Murray influenced the writing and speaking of English. He opposed the dropping of the final g in words like singing, which had been defended as easier on the ear, and a reaction against the practice began in the 1820s. He opposed the dropping of the initial h, and the ending of sentences with weak words like prepositions, and his preferences have become commonplaces of good practice. He was certainly widely accepted, and sometimes resented, as the arbiter of correctness and good style. Indeed it was remarked with some irony that it was an American from New York who 'taught England her grammar'.

Eloquent testimony to Murray's success is provided by the flood of adaptations, supplements and would-be improvements that poured from the presses between 1804 and 1877 – some 74 in all. Timothy Flint commented in 1835 on the American schoolmasters who published grammars in the hope 'of becoming the Lindley Murrays of their age'. Later times however were to require other approaches that were less coloured by the 18th-century models Murray had used. He had taken the first steps in making the needs of young pupils the primary consideration in designing their text-books, a process which was to lead ultimately to the dropping of formal grammar altogether from the teaching of English.

There have been many who felt that this was a serious loss, and the Secretary of State for Education has recently asked teachers 'to give greater emphasis to pupils' mastery of the grammatical structure of the English language'. Teachers in general resisted the idea of teaching grammar as a separate exercise, but accepted that teaching of grammatical structure should be given in the context of children's over-all development as language users (Report of the National Curriculum Council on the teaching of English, March 1989). The strenuous intellectual demands which Murray's system made would now be felt to be misplaced, but his aim of clarity in thinking, speaking and writing is as important as ever; we may even feel some nostalgia for his old-fashioned stress on elegance and style.

## ENGLISH GRAMMAR.

guage, ſtrictly ſpeaking, contains but ten ſimple vowel ſounds; to repreſent which, we have only five diſtinct characters or letters.

The following liſt will ſhow the ſounds of the conſonants, being in number twenty-two.

| | | | | |
|---|---|---|---|---|
| b | as | heard | in | bay, tub. |
| d | as | | in | day, fad. |
| f | as | | in | off, for. |
| v | as | | in | van, love. |
| g | as | | in | egg, go. |
| h *. | as | | in | hot. |
| k | as | | in | kill, oak. |
| l | as | | in | lap, all. |
| m | as | | in | my, mum. |
| n | as | | in | no, on. |
| p | as | | in | pit, map. |
| r | as | | in | rat, far. |
| ſ | as | | in | ſo, iſs. |
| z | as | | in | zed, buzz. |
| t | as | | in | to, mat. |
| w | as | | in | wo. |
| y | as | | in | ye. |
| ng | as | | in | ing. |
| ſh | as | | in | ſhy, aſh. |
| th | as | | in | thin. |
| th | as | | in | then. |
| zh | as | | in | viſion. |

Several letters marked in the Engliſh alphabet, as conſonants, are either ſuperfluous, or repreſent, not ſimple, but complex ſounds. C, for inſtance, is ſuperfluous in both its ſounds; the one being expreſſed by *k*, and the other by *s*. G, in the ſoft pronunciation, is not a ſimple, but a complex ſound; as *age* is pronounced *adge*. J is unneceſſary, becauſe its ſound, and that of the ſoft *g*, are in our lan-

---

* Some grammarians ſuppoſe *b* to mark only an aſpiration, or breathing: but it appears to be a diſtinct ſound, and formed in a particular manner, by the organs of ſpeech. *Encyclp. Britannica.*

*Page four of 1801 7th edition giving the sound of the consonants.*

CHAPTER VI

# Excerpts from the Grammar
(The seventh edition of 1801)

ENGLISH GRAMMAR is the art of speaking and writing the English language with propriety.[1] It is divided into four parts, viz.
ORTHOGRAPHY, ETYMOLOGY, SYNTAX and PROSODY.
    This division may be rendered more intelligible to young minds, by observing, in other words, that Grammar treats of the form and sound of the letters, the combination of the letters into syllables, and syllables into words; of the different sorts of words, their derivations, and various modifications; of the union and right order of words in the formation of a sentence; and of the just pronunciation, and poetical construction of sentences.[2]

PART I – ORTHOGRAPHY

Chapter I. Orthography teaches the nature and power of letters, and the just method of spelling words.
    A perfect alphabet of the English language, and, indeed, of every other language, would contain a number of letters, precisely equal to the number of simple articulate sounds belonging to the language. Every simple sound would have its distinct character; and that character be the representative of no other sound. But this is far from being the state of the English alphabet. It has more original sounds than distinct significant letters; and, consequently, some of these letters are made to represent, not one alone, but several sounds. This will appear by reflecting, that the sounds signified by the united letters *th, sh, ng,* are elementary, and have no single appropriate characters in our alphabet; and that the letters *a* and *u* represent the different sounds heard in *hat, hate, hall* and in *but, bull, mule.* . .

*A* has three sounds; the long or slender, the short or open, and the broad:
    The long; as in day, name, basin.
    The short; as in barrel, fancy, glass.
    The broad; as in call, wall, all.[3] . . .

*H.* The sound signified by this letter, is, as before observed, an articulate sound, and not merely an aspiration. It is heard in the words hat, horse, Hull. It is seldom mute at the beginning of a word. It is always silent after *r*; as rhetorick, rheum, rhubarb. H final, preceded by a vowel, is always silent, as, ah! hah! oh! soh! Sarah! Messiah.

From the faintness of the sound of this letter, in many words, and its total silence in others, added to the negligence of tutors, and the inattention of pupils, it has happened, that many persons have become almost incapable of acquiring its just and full pronunciation. It is therefore incumbent on teachers, to be particularly careful to inculcate a clear and distinct utterance of this sound on all proper occasions.[4] . . .

Chapter III. RULES for spelling.

Rule I. Monosyllables ending with *f, l,* or *s,* preceded by a single vowel, double the final consonant: as, staff, mill, pass, etc.
The only exceptions are, of, if, as, is, has, was, yes, his, this, us and thus. . . .

Rule X. When *ing* or *ish* are added to words ending with silent *e*, the *e* is almost invariably omitted: as, place, placing; lodge, lodging; slave, slavish; prude, prudish.

Rule XI. Words taken into composition, often drop those letters which were superfluous in their simples; as, handful, dunghil, withal, also, chilblain, foretel.

PART II – ETYMOLOGY

Chapter I. The second part of grammar is etymology,[5] which treats of the different sorts of words, their derivation, and the various modifications by which the sense of a primitive word is diversified.

There are in English nine sorts of words, or, as they are commonly called, PARTS of SPEECH; namely, the ARTICLE, the SUBSTANTIVE or NOUN, the PRONOUN, the ADJECTIVE, the VERB, the ADVERB, the PREPOSITION, the CONJUNCTION and the INTERJECTION. . .

Chapter III.[6] A SUBSTANTIVE or Noun is the name of anything that exists, or of which we have any notion; as, man, virtue, London, etc. . .

Proper names or substantives, are the names appropriated to individuals as, George, London, Thames.

Common names or substantives, stand for kinds containing many sorts, or for sorts containing many individuals under them; as, animal, man, tree, etc. . .

To substantives belong, gender, number and case. Gender is the distinction of sex. There are three genders, the MASCULINE, the FEMININE, and the NEUTER... Some substantives naturally neuter are, by a figure of speech, converted into the masculine or feminine gender; as, when we say of the sun, he is setting, and of a ship, she sails well, etc.

Figuratively, in the English tongue, we commonly give the masculine gender to nouns which are conspicuous for the attributes of imparting or communicating, and which are by nature strong and efficacious. Those again, are made feminine, which are conspicuous for the attributes of containing or bringing forth, or which are peculiarly beautiful or amiable. Upon these principles the sun is said to be masculine; and the moon, being the receptacle of the sun's light, to be feminine. The earth is generally feminine. A ship, a country, a city, etc. are likewise made feminine, being receivers or containers. Time is always masculine, on account of its mighty efficacy. Virtue is feminine from its beauty, and its being the object of love. Fortune and the church are generally put in the feminine gender.[7]

The cases of substantives signify their different terminations, which serve to express the relations of one thing to another. In English substantives have but two cases,[8] the nominative and possessive or genitive. The nominative case simply expresses the name of a thing, or the subject of the verb: as, 'The boy plays,' 'The girls learn.' The possessive or genitive case expresses the relation of property or possession; and has an apostrophe with the letter *s* coming after it: as, 'The scholar's duty.'... When the plural ends in *s*, the other *s* is omitted, but the apostrophe is retained: as, 'On eagles' wings.'

The English language, to express different connexions and relations of one thing to another, uses, for the most part, prepositions. The Greek and Latin among the ancient, and some too among the modern languages, as the German, vary the termination or ending of the substantive...

But though in the sentence, 'A wise man controls his passions,' we cannot properly say, that the noun 'passions' is in the objective case, and governed by the active verb, 'control', yet we may with propriety assert, that the noun 'passions' is the object of that active verb; and this may answer all the ends of parsing, and of showing the connexion and dependence of words under such circumstances...[9]

Chapter IV. A PRONOUN is a word used instead of a noun, to avoid the too frequent repetition of the same word: as 'The man is happy; he is benevolent, he is useful'. There are four kinds of pronouns, viz. the PERSONAL, the POSSESSIVE, the RELATIVE, and the ADJECTIVE PRONOUNS. There are five Personal Pronouns, viz. *I, thou, he, she, it*; with their plurals, *we, ye,* or *you, they*...

Chapter V. An Adjective is a word added to a substantive, to express its quality: as, 'An *industrious* man'; 'a *virtuous* woman'. . . The only variation which it admits, is that of degrees of comparison. There are commonly reckoned three degrees of comparison; the POSITIVE, COMPARATIVE and SUPERLATIVE. The Positive State expresses the quality of an object, without any increase of diminution; as, good, wise, great. The Comparative Degree increases or lessens the positive in signification; as, wiser, greater, less wise. The Superlative Degree increases or lessens the positive to the highest or lowest degree; as, wisest, greatest, least wise. . .[10]

Chapter VI. A VERB is a word which signifies to BE, to DO, or to SUFFER: as, 'I am, I rule, I am ruled.' Verbs are of three kinds; ACTIVE, PASSIVE and NEUTER. . . A Verb Active expresses an action, and necessarily implies an agent, and an object acted upon: as, to love, 'I love Penelope'. A Verb Passive expresses a passion or a suffering, or the receiving of an action; and necessarily implies an object acted upon, and an agent by which it is acted upon: as, to be loved; 'Penelope is loved by me'. A Verb Neuter expresses neither action nor passion, but being, or a state of being: as, 'I am, I sleep, I sit'.

The verb active is also called *transitive*, because the action passes over to the object, or has an effect upon some other thing: as, 'The tutor instructs his pupils'. . . Verbs neuter may properly be denominated *intransitives*, because the effect is confined within the agent, and does not pass over to any object. . .

Auxiliary or helping verbs, are those by the help of which the English verbs are principally conjugated. They are *do, be, have, shall, will, may, can*, with their variations; and *let* and *must*, which have no variations. . .

Mode or Mood is a particular form of the verb, showing the manner in which the being, action of passion is represented.

There are five moods of verbs, the INDICATIVE, the IMPERATIVE, the POTENTIAL, the SUBJUNCTIVE, and the INFINITIVE.

The Indicative Mood simply indicates or declares a thing: as 'He loves, he is loved': or it asks a question; as, 'Does he love?'

The Imperative Mood is used for commanding, exhorting, entreating, or permitting: as, 'Depart thou; mind ye; let us stay; go in peace.'

Though this mood derives its name from its intimation of command, it is used on occasions of a very opposite nature, even in the humblest supplications of an inferior being to one who is definitely his superior: as, 'Give us this day our daily bread.'[11]

The Potential Mood implies possibility or liberty, power, will, or obligation: as, 'It may rain; I can ride; he would walk; they should learn.'

The Subjunctive Mood represents a thing under a condition, motive, wish, supposition, etc.; and is preceded by a conjunction, expressed or understood, and attended by another verb: as, 'I will respect him, though he chide me'; 'Were he good, he would be happy:' that is, 'if he were good.'[12]

The Infinitive Mood expresses a thing in a general and unlimited manner, without any distinction of number or person; as, 'to act, to speak, to be feared.'. . .

The Participle is a certain form of the verb, and derives its name from its participating, not only of the properties of a verb, but also of those of an adjective: as, 'I am desirous of *knowing* him'; '*admired* and *applauded*, he became vain;' '*having finished* his work, he submitted it,' etc. . . .

The participle is distinguished from the adjective, by the former's expressing the idea of time, and the latter's denoting only a quality. The phrases, '*loving* to give as well as to receive,' '*moving* in haste,'. . . contain participles giving the idea of time; but the epithets contained in the expressions, 'a *loving* child,' 'a *moving* spectacle,'. . . mark simply the qualities referred to, without any regard to time; and may properly be called participial adjectives. . . Participles sometimes perform the office of substantives, and are used as such; as in the following instances: 'The *beginning*;' 'a good *understanding*;' '*excellent* writing.'. . .[13]

The auxiliary and neuter verb *To be*, is conjugated as follows: . . .[14]

Some writers of grammar assert, that there are no Passive Verbs in the English language, because we have not verbs of this kind with a peculiar termination, all of them being formed by the different tenses of the auxiliary *to be*, joined to the perfect participle of the verb. This is, however, to mistake the true nature of the English verb; and to regulate it, not on the principles of our own tongue, but on those of foreign languages. . . Even the Greek and Latin passive verbs require an auxiliary to conjugate some of their tenses. . .

The English tongue is, in many respects, materially different from the learned languages: and it is necessary to regard these peculiarities, when we are forming a system of English Grammar. It is therefore very possible to be mistaken ourselves, and to mislead and to perplex others, by an undistinguishing attachment to the principles and arrangement of the Greek and Latin Grammarians.

Chapter VIII.[15] Prepositions serve to connect words with one another, and to show the relation between them. They are, for the most part, set before nouns and pronouns: as, 'He went *from* London *to* York;' 'She is *above* disguise.' Prepositions are separable or inseparable. The separable prepositions are those which may be used separately from other words: as, 'above, about, over, under, at, after, with,' etc. Some of these are sometimes conjoined with other words: as, 'overtake, undertake, afterward.' The inseparable prepositions are used only in the composition of words: such as, *be, fore, mis,* etc.; 'Betimes, foretel, misconduct.'[16]

Chapter IX. A CONJUNCTION is a part of speech that is chiefly used to connect sentences; so as, out of two, to make one sentence. It sometimes connects only words. . . Relative pronouns, as well as conjunctions, serve to connect sentences: as, 'Blessed is the man *who* feareth the Lord, *and* keepeth his commandments.'[17]

Chapter X. INTERJECTIONS are words thrown in between the parts of a sentence, to express the passions or emotions of the speaker. . .

Those which intimate earnestness or grief, are, *O! oh! ah! alas!* Such as are expressive of contempt, are, *pish! tush!* Of wonder, *heigh! really! strange!* Of calling, *hem! ho! soho!* Of aversion or disgust, *foh! fie! away!* Of a call of the attention, *lo! behold! hark!* Of requesting silence, *hush! hist!* Of salutation, *welcome! hail! all hail!*

Chapter XI. . . . Words are derived from one another in various ways, viz.
1. Substantives are derived from verbs: as from 'to love' comes 'lover'. . .
2. Verbs are derived from substantives, adjectives and sometimes from adverbs, as from substantive *salt* comes 'to salt'; from the adjective *warm* 'to warm', and from the adverb *forward* 'to forward'. . .
3. Adjectives are derived from substantives, as from *health* 'healthy'. . .
4. Substantives are derived from adjectives, sometimes by adding the termination *ness*, as 'white whiteness', sometimes by adding *th* or *t*, and making a small change in some of the letters: as 'Long, length; high height.'
5. Adverbs of quality are derived from adjectives by adding *ly*. . .

There are so many ways of deriving words from one another, that it would be extremely difficult, and nearly impossible, to enumerate them. . .

That part of derivation which consists in tracing English words to the Saxon, Greek, Latin, French, and other languages must be omitted, as the English scholar is not supposed to be acquainted with these languages.[18] . . .

## Part III - SYNTAX

The third part of grammar is SYNTAX, which shows the agreement and right disposition of words in a sentence.

A sentence is an assemblage of words, expressed in proper form, ranged in proper order, and concurring to make a complete sense. . .[19]

The principal parts of a simple sentence are, the agent,[20] the attribute, and the object. The agent is the thing chiefly spoken of; the attribute is the thing or action affirmed or denied of it; and the object is the thing affected by such action. . .

Syntax principally consists of two parts, *Concord* and *Government*. Concord is the agreement which one word has with another, in gender, number, case, or person. Government is that power which one part of speech has over another, in directing its mood, tense, or case. To produce the agreement and right disposition of words in a sentence, many rules are necessary.

Rule I. A verb must agree with its nominative case, in number and person; as, 'I learn;' 'Thou art improved;' 'The birds sing.'

> The following are a few examples of the violation of this rule. 'There are a variety of virtues to be exercised;' 'there *is*.'. . . 'Scotland and thee did in each other live.' 'We are alone; here's no person but thee and I.' It ought in both places to be '*thou*', the nominative case to the verb expressed or understood: and *here are,* instead of *here's*. . .[21]

Rule IV. A noun of multitude, or signifying many, may have a verb or pronoun agreeing with it, either of the singular or plural number; yet not without regard to the import of the word, as conveying unity or plurality of idea: as, 'The meeting *was* large;' 'My people *do* not consider; *they* have not known me;' 'The council *were* divided in *their* sentiments.'

Rule V. Pronouns must always agree with their antecedents, and the nouns for which they stand, in gender, number, and person: as, 'This is the friend *whom* I love;' 'That is the vice *which* I hate.'. . .

> Many persons are apt, in conversation, to put the objective case of the personal pronouns, in the place of *these* and *those*: as, 'give me them books'; instead of '*those* books.'. . . In some dialects the word *what* is improperly used for *that*, and sometimes we find it in this sense in writing: 'They will never believe but *what* I have been entirely to blame,' instead of 'but *that*.'. . .

> We hardly consider little children as persons, because that term gives us the idea of reason and reflection: and therefore the application of the personal relative *who*, in this case, seems to be harsh. 'A child *who*'. It is still more improperly applied to animals.[22]. . .

Rule VIII.  . . . The adjective pronouns, *this* and *that*, etc. must agree in number, with their substantives: as 'This book, these books.'

A few instances of the breach of this rule are here exhibited. 'I have not travelled this twenty years;' '*these* twenty.' 'Those sort of people fear nothing;' '*that* sort.'. . .

The practice of the best and most correct writers, or a great majority of them, corroborated by general usage, forms, during its continuance, the standard of language; more especially, if, in particular instances, this practice continue, after objection and due consideration. . .

On this principle, many forms of expression, not less deviating from the general analogy of the language, than those before mentioned, are to be considered as strictly proper and justifiable. Of this kind are the following. '*None* of them *are* varied to express the gender;' and yet *none* originally signified *no one*. '*Himself* shall do the work;' here what was at first appropriated to the objective, is now properly used as the nominative case. . .[23]

Double comparatives and superlatives should be avoided: such as, 'A worser conduct;' 'The most straitest sect.' They should be, 'worse conduct'; 'the straitest sect.' Adjectives that have in them a superlative signification, do not properly admit of the superlative form superadded: such as, 'Chief, extreme, perfect, right, universal.'. . .

Rule XI.  Active verbs govern the objective case: as 'Truth ennobles *her*;' 'She comforts *me*.'

In English the nominative case, denoting the agent, usually goes before the verb; and the objective case, denoting the object, follows the verb active. But the pronoun, having a proper form for each of these cases, sometimes when it is in the objective case, follows the object and verb; as, '*Whom* ye ignorantly worship, *him* declare I unto you.' The position of the pronoun sometimes occasions its proper case and government to be neglected: as in the following instances: 'Who should I see the other day but my old friend?' 'Whoever the court favours.'[24, 25]

## A PRAXIS
## OR EXAMPLE OF GRAMMATICAL RESOLUTION[26]

'Patience and resolution will in due time be rewarded.'

*Patience*, a common substantive; *and*, a conjunction; *resignation*, a common substantive; *will be rewarded*, a verb in the passive voice, indicative mood, future tense, third person plural, agreeing with its nominative case, 'patience and resignation', according to RULE II (Two or more nouns, etc. in the singular number, joined together by one or more copulative conjunctions, must have verbs, nouns and pronouns agreeing with them in the plural number) and composed of the auxiliaries 'will be' and the perfect participle 'rewarded'; *in*, a preposition; *due*, an adjective; *time*, a common substantive of the singular number.

The preceding specimen of parsing will be sufficient to assist the learners in this business; and to enable them, in other exercises, to point out and apply most of the remaining rules.

## Part IV – PROSODY

... Punctuation is the art of dividing a written composition into sentences, or parts of sentences, by points or stops, for the purpose of marking the different pauses which the sense, and an accurate pronunciation require. The Comma represents the shortest pause; the Semicolon, a pause double that of the comma; the Colon, double that of the semicolon; and the Period, double that of the colon ...

The Dash, though often used improperly by hasty and incoherent writers, may be introduced with propriety, where the sentence breaks off abruptly; where a significant pause is required; or where there is an unexpected turn in the sentiment...[27,28]

## APPENDIX

PART I: PURITY of style consists in the use of such words, and such constructions, as belong to the idiom of the language which we speak; in opposition to words and phrases that are taken from other languages, or that are ungrammatical, obsolete, new-coined, or used without proper authority... The introduction of foreign and learned words, unless where necessity requires them, should never be admitted into our composition. Barren languages may need such assistance, but ours is not one of these. A multitude of Latin words, in particular, have, of late, been poured in upon our language. On some occasions they give an appearance of elevation and dignity to style; but they often render it stiff and apparently forced. In general, a plain, native style, is not only more intelligible to all readers, but by a proper management of words, it can be made equally strong and expressive with this Latinised English, or any foreign idioms.

PROPRIETY of language is the selection of such words as the best usage has appropriated to those ideas, which we intend to express by them; in opposition to low expressions, and to words and phrases which would be less significant of the ideas that we mean to convey. Style may be pure, that is, it may all be strictly English, without Scotticisms or Gallicisms, or ungrammatical irregular expressions of any kind, and may, nevertheless, be deficient in propriety: for the words may be ill chosen, not adapted to the subject, nor fully expressive of the author's sense.

To preserve propriety, therefore, we must...
1. Avoid low expressions: such as, 'Topsy turvy, currying favour, dancing attendance.'
2. Supply words that are wanting. 'This generous action greatly increased his former services'; it should have been, 'greatly increased *the merit* of his former services.'

3. In the same sentence, be careful not to use the same word too frequently, nor in different senses. . .
4. Avoid the injudicious use of technical terms. . .
5. Avoid equivocal or ambiguous words. . .
6. Avoid unintelligible and inconsistent words and phrases. . .

PRECISION signifies retrenching superfluities, and pruning the expression, so as to exhibit neither more nor less than an exact copy of the person's idea who uses it. . . To unite copiousness and precision, to be full and easy, and at the same time correct and exact in the choice of every word, is no doubt one of the highest and most difficult attainments in writing.

PART II: SENTENCES, in general, should neither be very long, nor very short: long ones require close attention to make us clearly perceive the connexion of the several parts; and short ones are apt to break the sense, and weaken the connexion of thought. A long succession of either long or short sentences should be avoided; for the ear tires of either of them when too long continued. . .

The first requisite of a perfect sentence is *Clearness*. Whatever leaves the mind in any sort of suspense as to the meaning, ought to be avoided. . .

The second requisite of a perfect sentence is its *Unity*. . . For the very nature of a sentence implies that one proposition is expressed. It may consist of parts, indeed, but these parts must be so closely bound together, as to make the impression upon the mind, of one object, not of many. . .

The third requisite of a perfect sentence, is, *Strength*. By this is meant such a disposition and management of the several words and members, as shall bring out the sense to the best advantage, and give every word, and every member its due weight and force. Any words which do not add some importance to the meaning of a sentence, always injure it. . . A weaker assertion or proposition should never come after a stronger one. When our sentence consists of two members, the longer should, generally, be the concluding one. Avoid concluding sentences with an adverb, a preposition, or any inconsiderable word. . . This must not be understood to refer to such words, when the stress and significancy of the sentence rest chiefly upon them. . . In order to give a sentence this proper close, the longest member of it, and the fullest words, should be reserved to the conclusion. . .

The fourth requisite of a perfect sentence, is a judicious use of *Figures of Speech*. . . In general, Figures of Speech imply some departure from simplicity of expression; the idea which we mean to convey is expressed in a particular manner, and with some circumstance added, which is designed to render the expression more strong and vivid. When I say for instance, 'That a good man enjoys comfort in the midst of adversity;' I just express my thoughts in the simplest manner possible: but when I say, 'To the upright there ariseth light in darkness;' the same sentiment is expressed in a figurative style; 'light' is put in the place of 'comfort', and 'darkness' is used to suggest the idea of 'adversity'. . . The principal advantages of figures of speech are the two following. *First*, they enrich language, and render it more copious... *Secondly*. They frequently give us a much clearer and more striking view of the principal object, than we could have, if it were expressed in simple terms...

A *Metaphor* is a figure founded entirely on the resemblance which one object bears to another... Care should be taken that the resemblance which is the foundation of the metaphor, be clear and perspicuous not far-fetched, nor difficult to discover... We should avoid making two inconsistent metaphors meet on one object. This is what is called a mixed metaphor, and is indeed one of the greatest misapplications of this figure...

A *Comparison* or *Simile*, is, when the resemblance between two objects is expressed in form, and generally pursued more fully than the nature of a metaphor admits: as when it is said, 'The actions of princes are like those of great rivers, the course of which every one beholds, but their springs have been seen by few.'... In comparisons of this nature, the understanding is concerned much more than the fancy: and therefore the rules to be observed, with respect to them, are, that they be clear, and that they be useful; that they tend to render our conception of the principal object more distinct; and that they do not lead our view aside, and bewilder it with any false light. We should always remember that similes are not arguments...[29]

Did we always think clearly, and were we at the same time fully masters of the language in which we write, there would be occasion for few rules. The understanding and language have a strict connexion; and they who are learning to compose and arrange their sentences with accuracy and order, are learning at the same time to think with accuracy and order; a consideration which alone will recompense the student for his attention to this branch of literature.

## *Notes* *Chapter VI*

[1] This is a wider sense than that which is now given to 'grammar'. cf. S. Johnson's definition (1790): 'the art of using words properly'.
[2] L.M. explains in the Introduction that 'the more important rules, definitions, and observations' are printed in larger type. These were to be memorised, and the rest, in smaller type, printed more closely, were to be studied later. *The Abridgement* consisted of the former alone.
[3] A fourth sound of A, 'the middle; as in far, farm, father' was added in later editions. 'Father' had originally been put in the 'short' category.
[4] Chapter II is on Syllables.
[5] L.M. does not restrict 'etymology' to the derivation of words, and was criticised for retaining the wider sense (*Eclectic Review* 1805).

[6] Chapter II is on Articles.
[7] Further discussion of gender was added later, from which the following is an extract: 'There appears to be a rational foundation for these figurative distinctions, though they have not been adopted in all countries. Many of the substances which in one language have masculine nouns have in others names that are feminine. The Greek and Latin and many of the modern tongues have nouns, some masculine, some feminine, which denote substances where sex never had existence. Nay, some languages are so defective in this respect as to class every object, inanimate as well as animate, under either the masculine or the feminine gender, as they have no neuter gender for those which are of neither sex.'
[8] L.M. later changed his mind and stated that English has three cases, 'the nominative, the possessive and the objective', adding that he 'long doubted the propriety of assigning to English substances an objective case'. He was aware that some teachers felt 'that it would be more intelligible to learners to consider the case of a noun as something different from its termination, and to suppose an objective case after verbs active and prepositions'. He pointed out that Greek and Latin have nouns where nominative and accusative have the same forms, and that a noun governed by an active verb 'is very differently circumstanced from a noun in the nominative or possessive case'.
[9] Murray's view on cases in English is original, being found in none of his predecessors. Sonnenschein (in Jesþersön, 1951, p. 177) praises him for liberating English grammar from the false definition of case, which he calls a 'monumental step'.
[10] He became stricter about comparison in later editions. Compare 'We say rightly, either "This is the weaker of the two" or "the weakest"' (1795) with 'We commonly say "This is the weaker of the two" or "the weakest", but the former appears to be preferable (or, is the regular mode of expression) because there are only two things compared' (1819).
[11] He later expanded this point: 'Even the name of imperative mood does not always correspond to its nature, for it sometimes petitions as well as commands. But . . . the practice of our grammarians is so uniformly fixed and so analogous to the languages, ancient and modern, which our youth have to study, that it would be an unwarrantable degree of innovation to deviate from the established terms and arrangements.
[12] He later attempted a clearer statement on the subjunctive: 'The general characteristic of this mood is contingency or uncertainty.' He divides it into 'doubt, condition, motive or end, wish, apprehension and supposition'.
[13] But he was not happy with the idea that words could be parsed differently if their functions differed. He rejects the suggestion that assertion is the essence of the verb, because this would mean that imperatives and infinitives are not verbs. 'The position is not tenable,' he says, 'that equivalence in sense implies solidarity in grammatical nature. . . This mode of reasoning would confound the acknowledged grammatical distinction of words. A pronoun, on this principle, may be proved to be a noun; a noun a verb; an adverb a noun and preposition. . . Thus in the sentence, 'I desire you to depart', the

words to depart may be called a noun, because they are equivalent in sense to the noun departure in the following sentence, 'I desire your departure.'
14 Then follows the full conjugation of to be, to have and to love.
15 Chapter VII is on adverbs.
16 Later he renounces inseparable prepositions: 'As they are not words of any kind, they cannot properly be called a species of prepositions.'
17 He later commented on the stylistic value of conjunctions: 'Conjunctions are those parts of language, which, by joining sentences in various ways, mark the connections and various dependences of human thought. And therefore if our thoughts be really connected and mutually dependent, it is most likely . . . that conjunctions will be employed to make that connexion and those dependences obvious to ourselves and to others. . . . As the fashionable mode of unconnected composition is less improving to the mind of the reader, so it promotes a habit of inaccuracy and negligence in a writer. . . . Conjunctions are not equally necessary in all sorts of writing. In poetry, where great conciseness of phrase is required and every appearance of formality avoided, many of them would have a bad effect. In passionate language too it may be proper to omit them. . . . And narrative will sometimes appear very graceful when the circumstances are plainly told with scarcely any other conjunction than the simple copulative and.
18 He later expanded his criticism of the use of etymology: 'Etymological deductions may certainly be pushed too far and valued too highly. . . Succeeding generations of men have an indubitable right to alter the old words of their predecessors, both in point of meaning and orthography, to make new ones, and to class the whole according to their own views and circumstances. . . Ancient usage is not the test by which the correctness of modern usage is to be tried.' But he objected to grammarians who liked introducing innovations: 'Observe a happy medium between too great and too little reverence for the usage of ancient times.'
19 His definition was later simplified to 'A sentence is an assemblage of words forming a complete sense.'
20 Later he substituted 'subject' for 'agent'.
21 Rules II and III also deal with the agreement of verbs with their subjects.
22 He follows Priestley in this view of children. Rules VI and VII deal with the form of the relative pronoun.
23 Rule IX deals with the articles, and Rule X with the possessive.
24 Such mistakes can be detected, L.M. suggested, by rephrasing as a statement, e.g. 'Whom do men say that I am' is wrong because as a statement it becomes 'Men say that I am he.' In 1795 he had suggested, 'Perhaps the objective case may also properly follow the word be, as "If it be me", "Should it be him"'. But later he adheres to the rule, 'The verb to be has the same case after it as that which next precedes it.'
25 Rules XII to XXII deal with the use of the infinitive, of tenses, of participles, of adverbs, of negatives, of prepositions, of conjunctions, of the subjunctive, of comparison and of ellipse.

[26] Later headed 'Directions for Parsing'. Nine other examples are given.
[27] Part IV also deals with pronunciation and with versification.
[28] Though he gave elaborate rules for punctuation, he later added the rider: 'Few precise rules can be given which will hold without exception; but much must be left to the judgement and taste of the writer.'
[29] He later added a third part to the Appendix on 'the great principle which decides the propriety of language'. He followed Campbell in his *Philosophy of Rhetoric* in stating the standard of correctness of usage in language to be 'reputable, national and present use'. 'Reputable' meant English as used by authors of reputation, general use being unacceptable as a standard as most people speak badly. 'National' excludes provincial or foreign uses.

# Index

ACKWORTH, 37, 46, 48, 50, 54, 61
Aims of publications, 29-31, 33
Alexander, Ann (Tuke), 36-7, 48
Animals, 4-5, 15, 35

BIBLE, 2, 41-2, 55, 56, 59-61
Business, 5, 11-12, 15-16, 25, 49-50, 60

CHARITABLE WORK, 31, 41-2, 46, 48, 56, 60
Classics, 9, 38, 48, 66
*Compendium*, 50, 56, 58-60
Copyright, sale of, 31, 38, 49-50

ECUMENICAL attitude, 26, 42, 55-60
Education, 4, 6, 9-12, 46-8, 56, 59-60
England, visits to, 4, 12-13, 20-1
*English Grammar*, viii-ix, xiii, 27-9, 31-3, 37, 38, 44, 70, CHAPS. V, VI
 Abridgement of, xiii, 29, 38, 66, 81
 aims of, 27, 31-3
 *Exercises* and *Key*, 27, 29
*English Reader*, 29, 30
 *Introduction* and *Sequel*, 30, 31

FRANK, Elizabeth, xiii, 30, 34-5, 37-8, 39-40, 42, 44, 46, 52
Future Life, 20, 26, 33, 46

GOUGH, John, vii, viii, x
Grammatical issues:
 cases, 67, 68, 73, 82

 criteria, 66-9, 77-8, 84
 etymology, 72, 83
 gender, 67, 73, 82
 Greek and Latin, 66-8, 75, 79
 influence, 68-9
 parsing, 3, 67, 68, 78-9, 82
 prescriptive attitude, 68
 punctuation, 68, 79, 84
 style, xiii, 79-81, 83
 tenses, 67

HEALTH, 9, 14-15, 16-20, 22-6, 29, 36, 40f., 50-2
Holgate House (Holdgate), 21-3, 36, 44, 52, 53, 54, 61-4

LAW, 10-12, 13-15, 41, 44, 49-50
*Lecteur François*, 30, 31
 *Introduction au Lecteur François*, 30, 31

MAIL, 7, 49-50
Marriage, 12, 35
Medicine, 19-20, 46, 64
Meetings for Worship, 25, 36, 44, 50, 52, 55, 56, 59, 60
*Memoir*, xiii, 39, 42
Ministers, Recorded, 20, 36, 46, 48, 61
Murray, Hannah, 12-13, 25, 35, 40, 41 44, 50, 52, 61, 62, 64, 65
Murray, Lindley, parents of:
 Mary, 1-3, 7, 8, 12-13, 34

85

Robert, 1-3, 5-6, 10-11, 13, 15,
   17, 19, 25, 34-36, 50
siblings of:
   Beulah, 2, 17, 35
   John, 2, 25, 35, 36, 46, 48-50,
      52
   Mary, 2, 33, 38, 46, 58
   Susannah, 2, 35, 46
Murray Trust, 42, 44

NEW YORK Meetings, 34, 35, 36, 48

PERKINS, Mary, 46, 47
Politics, 42, 45, 48-9
*Power of Religion on the Mind*, 25-6, 42, 55
Property, 49-50
Publisher-Booksellers, 26, 32, 36, 38, 46, 50
Purity in books, 27, 29-30, 38

QUAKER business, 5, 10-11, 15-16, 34-6, 38, 42, 49, 61
Quakerism, 21, 42, 49, CHAP. IV

RELIGION, 9-10, 20-1, 29, 30, 33-4, 49, 56, 58

God, 2, 12, 16, 20-1, 26-7, 34, 55, 58
Christ, 34, 38, 58
Religious Society of Friends, 2, 13-14, 42, CHAP. IV.
Revision of books, 27, 29, 31, 42
Richardson, Hannah, 62, 65
Robertson, Judith, 46, 54

SALE of books, 31, 38, 50
Schools, 3, 6, 34, 36, 38, 42, 46, 48, 50, 56
Schooling, 3, 6-9, 34, 66-7
*Spelling Book*, 30, 31
Summer house, 44, 62

TRINITY Lane School, xii, xiii, 36-8, 42, 44, 56
Tuke – Ann, 36, 48
   Esther, xiii, 36, 61
   Samuel, 36, 45, 61, 64
   William, 36, 37, 45

WAR of Independence, 14-15, 34, 35
Wilberforce, William, ix, 45

*'LIBERTY MAKES ME FAITHFUL'*
Believed traditionally to be the seal of Lindley Murray.